Keynes: A Very Short Introduction

VERY SHORT INTRODUCTIONS are for anyone wanting a stimulating and accessible way in to a new subject. They are written by experts, and have been published in more than 25 languages worldwide.

The series began in 1995, and now represents a wide variety of topics in history, philosophy, religion, science, and the humanities. The VSI library now contains over 200 volumes—a Very Short Introduction to everything from ancient Egypt and Indian philosophy to conceptual art and cosmology—and will continue to grow to a library of around 300 titles.

Very Short Introductions available now:

ADVERTISING   Winston Fletcher
AFRICAN HISTORY   John Parker and
   Richard Rathbone
AMERICAN POLITICAL PARTIES
   AND ELECTIONS   L. Sandy Maisel
THE AMERICAN
   PRESIDENCY   Charles O. Jones
ANARCHISM   Colin Ward
ANCIENT EGYPT   Ian Shaw
ANCIENT PHILOSOPHY
   Julia Annas
ANCIENT WARFARE
   Harry Sidebottom
ANGLICANISM   Mark Chapman
THE ANGLO-SAXON AGE
   John Blair
ANIMAL RIGHTS   David DeGrazia
ANTISEMITISM   Steven Beller
THE APOCRYPHAL GOSPELS
   Paul Foster
ARCHAEOLOGY   Paul Bahn
ARCHITECTURE   Andrew Ballantyne
ARISTOTLE   Jonathan Barnes
ART HISTORY   Dana Arnold
ART THEORY   Cynthia Freeland
ATHEISM   Julian Baggini
AUGUSTINE   Henry Chadwick
AUTISM   Uta Frith
BARTHES   Jonathan Culler
BESTSELLERS   John Sutherland
THE BIBLE   John Riches
BIBLICAL ARCHEOLOGY
   Eric H. Cline

BIOGRAPHY   Hermione Lee
THE BOOK OF MORMON
   Terryl Givens
THE BRAIN   Michael O'Shea
BRITISH POLITICS   Anthony Wright
BUDDHA   Michael Carrithers
BUDDHISM   Damien Keown
BUDDHIST ETHICS   Damien Keown
CAPITALISM   James Fulcher
CATHOLICISM   Gerald O'Collins
THE CELTS   Barry Cunliffe
CHAOS   Leonard Smith
CHOICE THEORY   Michael Allingham
CHRISTIAN ART   Beth Williamson
CHRISTIAN ETHICS
   D. Stephen Long
CHRISTIANITY   Linda Woodhead
CITIZENSHIP   Richard Bellamy
CLASSICAL MYTHOLOGY
   Helen Morales
CLASSICS   Mary Beard and
   John Henderson
CLAUSEWITZ   Michael Howard
THE COLD WAR   Robert McMahon
COMMUNISM   Leslie Holmes
CONSCIOUSNESS   Susan Blackmore
CONTEMPORARY ART
   Julian Stallabrass
CONTINENTAL PHILOSOPHY
   Simon Critchley
COSMOLOGY   Peter Coles
THE CRUSADES
   Christopher Tyerman

CRYPTOGRAPHY Fred Piper
  and Sean Murphy
DADA AND SURREALISM
  David Hopkins
DARWIN Jonathan Howard
THE DEAD SEA SCROLLS
  Timothy Lim
DEMOCRACY Bernard Crick
DESCARTES Tom Sorell
DESERTS Nick Middleton
DESIGN John Heskett
DINOSAURS David Norman
DIPLOMACY Joseph M. Siracusa
DOCUMENTARY FILM
  Patricia Aufderheide
DREAMING J. Allan Hobson
DRUGS Leslie Iversen
DRUIDS Barry Cunliffe
THE EARTH Martin Redfern
ECONOMICS Partha Dasgupta
EGYPTIAN MYTH Geraldine Pinch
EIGHTEENTH-CENTURY BRITAIN
  Paul Langford
THE ELEMENTS Philip Ball
EMOTION Dylan Evans
EMPIRE Stephen Howe
ENGELS Terrell Carver
EPIDEMIOLOGY Roldolfo Saracci
ETHICS Simon Blackburn
THE EUROPEAN UNION
  John Pinder and Simon Usherwood
EVOLUTION Brian and Deborah
  Charlesworth
EXISTENTIALISM Thomas Flynn
FASCISM Kevin Passmore
FASHION Rebecca Arnold
FEMINISM Margaret Walters
FILM MUSIC Kathryn Kalinak
THE FIRST WORLD WAR
  Michael Howard
FORENSIC PSYCHOLOGY
  David Canter
FORENSIC SCIENCE Jim Fraser
FOSSILS Keith Thomson

FOUCAULT Gary Gutting
FREE SPEECH Nigel Warburton
FREE WILL Thomas Pink
FRENCH LITERATURE John D. Lyons
THE FRENCH REVOLUTION
  William Doyle
FREUD Anthony Storr
FUNDAMENTALISM
  Malise Ruthven
GALAXIES John Gribbin
GALILEO Stillman Drake
GAME THEORY Ken Binmore
GANDHI Bhikhu Parekh
GEOGRAPHY John Matthews and
  David Herbert
GEOPOLITICS Klaus Dodds
GERMAN LITERATURE
  Nicholas Boyle
GERMAN PHILOSOPHY
  Andrew Bowie
GLOBAL CATASTROPHES
  Bill McGuire
GLOBAL WARMING Mark Maslin
GLOBALIZATION Manfred Steger
THE GREAT DEPRESSION AND
  THE NEW DEAL Eric Rauchway
HABERMAS
  James Gordon Finlayson
HEGEL Peter Singer
HEIDEGGER Michael Inwood
HIEROGLYPHS Penelope Wilson
HINDUISM Kim Knott
HISTORY John H. Arnold
THE HISTORY OF ASTRONOMY
  Michael Hoskin
THE HISTORY OF LIFE
  Michael Benton
THE HISTORY OF MEDICINE
  William Bynum
THE HISTORY OF TIME
  Leofranc Holford-Strevens
HIV/AIDS Alan Whiteside
HOBBES Richard Tuck
HUMAN EVOLUTION
  Bernard Wood

HUMAN RIGHTS
  Andrew Clapham
HUME   A. J. Ayer
IDEOLOGY   Michael Freeden
INDIAN PHILOSOPHY
  Sue Hamilton
INFORMATION   Luciano Floridi
INNOVATION
  Mark Dodgson and David Gann
INTELLIGENCE   Ian J. Deary
INTERNATIONAL
  MIGRATION   Khalid Koser
INTERNATIONAL
  RELATIONS   Paul Wilkinson
ISLAM   Malise Ruthven
ISLAMIC HISTORY
  Adam Silverstein
JOURNALISM   Ian Hargreaves
JUDAISM   Norman Solomon
JUNG   Anthony Stevens
KABBALAH   Joseph Dan
KAFKA   Ritchie Robertson
KANT   Roger Scruton
KEYNES   Robert Skidelsky
KIERKEGAARD   Patrick Gardiner
THE KORAN   Michael Cook
LANDSCAPES AND
  GEOMORPHOLOGY
  Andrew Goudie and Heather Viles
LAW   Raymond Wacks
THE LAWS OF THERMODYNAMICS
  Peter Atkins
LEADERSHIP   Keith Grint
LINCOLN   Allen C. Guelzo
LINGUISTICS   Peter Matthews
LITERARY THEORY   Jonathan Culler
LOCKE   John Dunn
LOGIC   Graham Priest
MACHIAVELLI   Quentin Skinner
THE MARQUIS DE SADE
  John Phillips
MARX   Peter Singer
MATHEMATICS   Timothy Gowers
THE MEANING OF LIFE
  Terry Eagleton

MEDICAL ETHICS   Tony Hope
MEDIEVAL BRITAIN
  John Gillingham and
  Ralph A. Griffiths
MEMORY   Jonathan K. Foster
MODERN ART   David Cottington
MODERN CHINA   Rana Mitter
MODERN IRELAND   Senia Pašeta
MODERN JAPAN
  Christopher Goto-Jones
MODERNISM   Christopher Butler
MOLECULES   Philip Ball
MORMONISM
  Richard Lyman Bushman
MUSIC   Nicholas Cook
MYTH   Robert A. Segal
NATIONALISM   Steven Grosby
NELSON MANDELA
  Elleke Boehmer
NEOLIBERALISM
  Manfred Steger and Ravi Roy
THE NEW TESTAMENT
  Luke Timothy Johnson
THE NEW TESTAMENT AS
  LITERATURE   Kyle Keefer
NEWTON   Robert Iliffe
NIETZSCHE   Michael Tanner
NINETEENTH-CENTURY
  BRITAIN   Christopher Harvie
  and H. C. G. Matthew
THE NORMAN
  CONQUEST   George Garnett
NORTH AMERICAN INDIANS
  Michael Green
NORTHERN IRELAND
  Marc Mulholland
NOTHING   Frank Close
NUCLEAR WEAPONS
  Joseph M. Siracusa
THE OLD TESTAMENT
  Michael D. Coogan
PARTICLE PHYSICS   Frank Close
PAUL   E. P. Sanders
PHILOSOPHY   Edward Craig
PHILOSOPHY OF LAW
  Raymond Wacks

PHILOSOPHY OF SCIENCE
  Samir Okasha
PHOTOGRAPHY Steve Edwards
PLATO Julia Annas
POLITICAL PHILOSOPHY
  David Miller
POLITICS Kenneth Minogue
POSTCOLONIALISM
  Robert Young
POSTMODERNISM
  Christopher Butler
POSTSTRUCTURALISM
  Catherine Belsey
PREHISTORY Chris Gosden
PRESOCRATIC PHILOSOPHY
  Catherine Osborne
PRIVACY Raymond Wacks
PROGRESSIVISM Walter Nugent
PSYCHIATRY Tom Burns
PSYCHOLOGY Gillian Butler and
  Freda McManus
PURITANISM Francis J. Bremer
THE QUAKERS Pink Dandelion
QUANTUM THEORY
  John Polkinghorne
RACISM Ali Rattansi
THE REAGAN REVOLUTION
  Gil Troy
THE REFORMATION
  Peter Marshall
RELATIVITY Russell Stannard
RELIGION IN AMERICA
  Timothy Beal
THE RENAISSANCE Jerry Brotton
RENAISSANCE ART
  Geraldine A. Johnson
ROMAN BRITAIN Peter Salway
THE ROMAN EMPIRE
  Christopher Kelly
ROMANTICISM Michael Ferber
ROUSSEAU Robert Wokler
RUSSELL A. C. Grayling
RUSSIAN LITERATURE
  Catriona Kelly

THE RUSSIAN REVOLUTION
  S. A. Smith
SCHIZOPHRENIA
  Chris Frith and Eve Johnstone
SCHOPENHAUER
  Christopher Janaway
SCIENCE AND RELIGION
  Thomas Dixon
SCOTLAND Rab Houston
SEXUALITY Véronique Mottier
SHAKESPEARE Germaine Greer
SIKHISM Eleanor Nesbitt
SOCIAL AND CULTURAL
  ANTHROPOLOGY
  John Monaghan and Peter Just
SOCIALISM Michael Newman
SOCIOLOGY Steve Bruce
SOCRATES C. C. W. Taylor
THE SOVIET UNION
  Stephen Lovell
THE SPANISH CIVIL WAR
  Helen Graham
SPANISH LITERATURE
  Jo Labyani
SPINOZA Roger Scruton
STATISTICS David J. Hand
STUART BRITAIN John Morrill
SUPERCONDUCTIVITY
  Stephen Blundell
TERRORISM Charles Townshend
THEOLOGY David F. Ford
THOMAS AQUINAS Fergus Kerr
TACQUEVILLE
  Harvey C. Mansfield
TRAGEDY Adrian Poole
THE TUDORS John Guy
TWENTIETH-CENTURY BRITAIN
  Kenneth O. Morgan
THE UNITED NATIONS
  Jussi M. Hanhimäki
THE U.S. CONGRESS
  Donald A. Ritchie
UTOPIANISM
  Lyman Tower Sargent

THE VIKINGS   Julian Richards
WITCHCRAFT   Malcolm Gaskill
WITTGENSTEIN   A. C. Grayling
WORLD MUSIC   Philip Bohlman

THE WORLD TRADE
  ORGANIZATION
  Amrita Narlikar
WRITING AND SCRIPT
  Andrew Robinson

Available soon:

ENGLISH LITERATURE
  Jonathan Bate
AGNOSTICISM   Robin Le Poidevin
ARISTOCRACY   William Doyle

MARTIN LUTHER   Scott H. Hendrix
MICHAEL FARADAY
  Frank. A. J. L. James

For more information visit our web site
www.oup.co.uk/general/vsi/

Robert Skidelsky

KEYNES

A Very Short Introduction

OXFORD
UNIVERSITY PRESS

OXFORD

UNIVERSITY PRESS

Great Clarendon Street, Oxford OX2 6DP

Oxford University Press is a department of the University of Oxford.
It furthers the University's objective of excellence in research, scholarship,
and education by publishing worldwide in

Oxford New York

Auckland Cape Town Dar es Salaam Hong Kong Karachi
Kuala Lumpur Madrid Melbourne Mexico City Nairobi
New Delhi Shanghai Taipei Toronto

With offices in

Argentina Austria Brazil Chile Czech Republic France Greece
Guatemala Hungary Italy Japan Poland Portugal Singapore
South Korea Switzerland Thailand Turkey Ukraine Vietnam

Oxford is a registered trade mark of Oxford University Press
in the UK and in certain other countries

Published in the United States
by Oxford University Press Inc., New York

© Robert Skidelsky 2010

British Library Cataloguing in Publication Data

Data available

Library of Congress Cataloging in Publication Data

Data available

Typeset by SPI Publisher Services, Pondicherry, India
Printed in Great Britain by
Ashford Colour Press Ltd, Gosport, Hampshire

ISBN 978-0-19-959164-0

1 3 5 7 9 10 8 6 4 2

To William

Contents

Acknowledgements xiii

Introduction: The man and economist 1

1 The life 14

2 Keynes's philosophy of practice 38

3 The monetary reformer 55

4 *The General Theory* 79

5 Economic statesmanship 103

6 Keynes's legacy 120

Epilogue: The view from 2010 146

References 171

Further reading 181

Index 185

Acknowledgements

I would like to thank Peter Oppenheimer, Liam Halligan, and Clive Lennox for their incisive comments. All the imperfections are mine.

Introduction: The man and economist

Keynes's fundamental insight was that we do not know – cannot calculate – what the future will bring. In such a world, money offers psychological security against uncertainty. When savers become pessimistic about future prospects they can decide to hoard their savings rather than invest them in businesses. Thus there is no guarantee that all income earned will be spent. This amounts to saying that there is no natural tendency for all available resources to be employed. 'Men cannot be employed', he wrote in *The General Theory*:

> when the object of desire (i.e. money) is something which cannot be produced [employ people in its production] and the demand for which cannot be readily choked off. There is no remedy but to persuade the public that green cheese is practically the same thing and to have a green cheese factory (i.e. a central bank) under public control.

When Keynes talked about money rather than goods being the 'object of desire', was he being frivolous or was he saying something profound in a playful way? How seriously was one to take his suggestion that one should make money go bad, like 'green cheese'?

People have debated these matters ever since. Was Keynes merely a speculator in ideas or was he a saviour who brought a diseased world a new hope of health? The Fabian Beatrice Webb wrote: 'Keynes is not serious about economic problems; he plays a game of chess with it in his leisure hours. The only serious cult with him is aesthetics.' To Russell Leffingwell, a US Treasury official who negotiated with Keynes at the Paris Peace Conference in 1919, Keynes was 'always perverse, Puckish . . . a bright boy, shocking his admiring elders by questioning the existence of God, and the Ten Commandments!' However, for the economist James Meade, who knew him both as a postgraduate at Cambridge and as a civil servant in the war, Keynes 'was not merely a very great man; he was a very good man also'. For young economists generally, *The General Theory* shone out as a beacon of light in a benighted world. 'What we got was joyful revelation in dark time,' recalled David Bensusan-Butt, who came up to read economics at King's College, Cambridge, in 1933. 'Keynes's reformed capitalism had everything and more the Fabian generation had looked for in socialism: it was morally speaking egalitarian, it was fully employed, it was generous and gay. . . .' Another student, Lorie Tarshis, wrote: 'And finally what Keynes supplied was *hope*: hope that prosperity could be restored and maintained without the support of prison camps, executions and bestial interrogations. . . .'

These stereotypes have persisted. To anti-Keynesians Keynes is someone who produced fertile, but ultimately unsound and distracting hypotheses; to Keynesians he offered a profound insight into the way economies behave, permanently valuable tools of economic policy. The stereotypes are true but incomplete. Keynes had many sides; different people saw different aspects of him. He also changed, so that different generations saw him in different lights. He did love to play with ideas in a reckless way, but, as his friend Oswald Falk remarked, 'in this manner, in spite of false scents, he caught up with the march of events more rapidly than did others'. He was a striking phrase-maker, and used words deliberately to rouse people from their mental torpor. But 'when the seats of power and authority have been attained there should be no more poetic licence'. About his ultimate seriousness of purpose there can be no real doubt. The real question is whether the concepts he bequeathed were the right ones to make sense of his world, and beyond that, of our world.

Keynes's ideas were rooted in time and place. He was born in 1883 and died in 1946. He was born into a world which assumed peace, prosperity, and progress to be the natural order of things, and lived long enough to see all these expectations toppled. When he grew up, Britain was the centre of a mighty empire: in the last months of his life he was handing round the begging bowl in Washington. His life spanned not just the collapse of British power, but the growing enfeeblement of the British economy. It spanned the passage from certainty to uncertainty, from the perfumed garden of his youth to the jungle of his mature years, where monsters prowled. In 1940, he wrote to an American correspondent: 'For the first time for more than two centuries Hobbes has more message for us than Locke'.

Keynes was a product of decaying Victorian conventions. This is what made the problem of behaviour, personal and social, so central for him. But before the First World War this very decay produced a great surge of cheerfulness in Keynes and his contemporaries. They saw themselves as the first generation freed from Christian 'hocus-pocus', the creators and beneficiaries of a new Enlightment, who could work out their ideals and maxims of conduct in the pure light of reason. Their ideals were aesthetic and personal; public life was rather depressing, because the great victories of progress, it seemed, had all been won. Experiment was the order of the day in the arts, in philosophy, in science, and in life-styles, rather than in politics or economics. Diaghilev was born in 1872, Picasso in 1881, Gropius in 1883, James Joyce and Virginia Woolf in 1882, Russell in 1872, G. E. Moore in 1873, Wittgenstein in 1889, Einstein in 1880. Only Freud, of those who moulded early 20th-century consciousness, comes from an earlier generation, born in 1856.

Then came the First World War, and everything changed. After 1914 there was the management of the world to attend to – a world which, after 1914, seemed to be spinning into chaos. Here the problem was one of control, not liberation. Civilization, Keynes acknowledged in 1938, was a 'thin and precarious crust'. The men of power took over, determined to impose their versions of order on chaos: Stalin was born in 1879, Mussolini in 1883, Hitler in 1889. Modernism lost its innocence, as playfulness gave way to horror. And Keynes began to wonder about his early creed. 'I begin to see', he said to Virginia Woolf in 1934, 'that our generation – yours & mine ... owed a great deal to our fathers' religion. And the young ... who are brought up without it, will never get so much out of life. They're trivial: like dogs in their lusts. We had the best of both worlds. We destroyed Xty & yet had its benefits.' But the important point is that he never succumbed to the politics of cultural despair. Despite everything, that Edwardian cheerfulness survived. Uncertainty could be managed, not by brute force, but by brains, by the exercise of intelligence, and gradually the harmonies might be restored. This was his ultimate credo, his message, if there is one, for our time.

He was well qualified to convey it. Bertrand Russell has written that 'Keynes's intellect was the sharpest and clearest that I have ever known. When I argued with him, I felt that I took my life in my hands, and I seldom emerged without feeling something of a fool.' Others, like Kenneth Clark, felt he used his brilliance too unsparingly: 'he never dimmed his headlights'. But it was his liquidity of mind which chiefly struck his contempories: its tendency, as Kingsley Martin put it, to 'run round and over an obstacle rather than dispose of it. Like a stream he often appears travelling in opposite directions.' The jibe that wherever five economists were gathered there were six opinions and two of them were Keynes's was already familiar in his lifetime. 'But the charges of caprice and inconsistency so often levelled against him signify very little,' Kingsley Martin wrote, 'except that his mind deals swiftly and somewhat cavalierly with practical difficulties, offering one possible solution after another in a way that is terrifying and bewildering to the cautious and solidly rooted.' The irony, as Kurt Singer noted, was that someone who 'seemed to find rest only in motion ... [able] to build and to discard in one afternoon a memorable number of equally attractive conceptual schemes' should have bequeathed to the world 'the Book of a new faith'.

Yet it would be wrong to say of him, as he said of Lloyd George, that he was 'rooted in nothing'. He was born a Victorian, and traces of 'Victorian values' remained with him throughout. He had a strong inherited sense of duty, even though, like Sidgwick, he found it difficult to justify it philosophically. He believed in government by a benevolent clerisy, or intellectual aristocracy. There was in this notion a mingling of the social and intellectual which reflects the very Victorian rise of Keynes's own family, through brains and business acumen, into the circle of the governing class. He was a 'thinking' patriot, though his patriotism was free of any trace of jingoism. He was a firm believer in the virtues of the *Pax Britannica* and reluctant to believe that any other country could take on Britain's world role. He was pro-German, anti-French – another 19th-century inheritance.

Nonconformity was a powerful factor in Keynes's formation. It comes out in his frugality. People found his entertainments 'very economical', and at the end of his life he regretted he had not drunk more champagne. He became very wealthy, but he lived comfortably, not grandly or ostentatiously. As an economist, his imagination was much more excited by people's propensity to hoard than to splash; and he would turn this cultural, or psychological, defect in his own class background into a paradoxical explanation of why capitalist economies could run down.

He came from a family of preachers, especially on his mother's side. He was of the first generation of unbelievers untroubled by 'doubts', but theology was in his bones, and the distance between theology and economics much less than it is today. He had to the full the Nonconformist capacity for indignation and protest; his economic essays are secularized sermons. The 'unsurpassed individualism of our philosophy', to which he referred in 1938, rested on the belief that human beings (at least in England) had been sufficiently moralized by Victorian values that they could be 'safely released from the outward restraints of convention and traditional standards and inflexible rules of conduct, and left, from now onwards, to their own sensible devices, pure motives and reliable intuitions of the good'.

Keynes's social sympathies were not wide, though they widened as he grew older. His family had pulled themselves up by their bootstraps, and in general he expected others to do the same, provided there were enough jobs to go round. For the residue there was the Charity Organisation Society, and other typical mid-Victorian associations for helping the unfit and alcoholic. Keynes's hereditary Nonconformity was weakened by social acceptance. He had been to Eton, as a Colleger (as Eton scholars are called), and was increasingly at his happiest in the company of clever Old Etonians. He enjoyed the company of the rich and well-born, though he indulged it sparingly. As he grew older Keynes became more conservative, an apostle of continuity and evolutionary change. The social conclusions to which his economics pointed, he wrote at the end of *The General Theory*, were 'moderately conservative'. Capitalism, for which he had a moral distaste, could survive, under improved management.

What remained intact from his childhood were his work habits. Keynes was one of the most efficient working machines ever created. Thus he imposed his own order on a disorderly world. It enabled him to lead as many lives as he did, and to show zest for each one. Every nook and cranny of the day was packed with multifarious activities and projects. He got through all his business with astonishing expedition. He had an amazing capacity to switch from one thing to another; and despite all he did he seemed unhurried, with plenty of time for friendship, conversation, and hobbies.

It was Keynes's 'queer imaginative ardour about history, humanity' which endeared him to Virginia Woolf, his 'mind working always', overflowing 'vigorously into byepaths'. He had a universal curiosity, and could not touch any topic without weaving a theory about it, however fanciful. 'England could not have afforded Shakespeare had he been born fifty years earlier,' was one favourite saying. This attractive habit of rushing in where slower minds feared to tread, and relying on quick invention to get him out of tight corners, often affronted experts and gave him the reputation of an amateur, even in economics. But it was not all after-dinner chatter. Keynes could get totally obsessed by intellectual concerns apparently remote from the mainstream of his work. Early in life, he tried to work out a formula for predicting colour-blindness, based on Mendelian genetics; in the 1920s, he succumbed repeatedly to his 'Babylonian madness' – an essay on the origins of money. 'It is purely absurd and quite useless,' he wrote to Lydia Lopokova on 18 January 1924, 'But just as before I became absorbed in it to the point of frenzy . . . The result is I feel quite mad and silly. With a lunatic kiss and a wild eye, Maynard.'

Even his efficiency could not save him from constant fatigue. He was always overworked. As a young man he went to spend a restful weekend with the Russells, and twenty-six unexpected guests arrived, most of them, Russell implies, summoned by Keynes. Later in life brief-cases full of paper always accompanied him on his holidays abroad. He spent years of what he himself called 'Chinese torture' on college and university committees from which he could easily have escaped. 'Is it necessary?' 'Why do we buzz and fuzz?' 'Why do I do it?' Did Keynes have any identity in solitude? He does not give the impression of being at ease with himself. He thought he was ugly. He loathed his voice. His Bloomsbury friends complained of his lack of fastidiousness, and mocked his taste in pictures and furniture. The 'masks' which he put on were physical as well as mental. The playful eyes and sensuous mouth were covered up by the conventional disguises – the military moustache, the dark suits and Homburgs which he wore even on picnics – of the 'man of affairs'. He sought his identity in mastery of the external world.

In his attitude to his fellow humans, Keynes was a mixture of benevolence and intolerance. He had a great capacity for affection, and, unlike most fellow members of the Bloomsbury Group, was exceptionally loyal to his friends. He appreciated mental quirks, oddities, obsessions, which he often saw as containing interesting possibilities. He revered genius, a word which he used in its original sense of a 'free spirit'. Like many intellectuals he respected practical expertise, even of the humblest. He was quick to excuse the faults of youth and inexperience. He was not a patient man, but he could take enormous trouble with the affairs of his friends, and those he thought deserving of it.

At the same time he could be devastatingly rude – especially to those he thought ought to know better. He had the curse of Oxbridge, believing that all the cleverness of the world was located in it and its products. With this went a profoundly Anglocentric view of the world, more typical then than now. He often got away with rudeness because of his ready command of repartee and the technique of *reductio ad absurdum*. But he could also wound. The American economist Walter Stewart wrote that

> In conversation Keynes was frequently brilliant and not infrequently unkind. He could not resist scoring a point and would look around the circle of listeners to see whether others had noticed the arrow hit the mark. Some of his sharpest wit was used against those who could not easily defend themselves and even against the absent.

It was not a style calculated to endear. The Americans never took to it. Keynes's 'Open Letter' to Roosevelt in 1933, sounded, writes Herbert Stein, 'like the letter from a school teacher to the very rich father of a very dull pupil'. In Savannah, in March 1946, for the inaugural meeting of the International Monetary Fund, Keynes made a speech in which he hoped that 'there is no malicious fairy, no Carabosse' who had not been invited to the party. The reference was to Tchaikovsky's ballet, *Sleeping Beauty*, but Frederic Vinson the US Secretary of the Treasury, took it personally. 'I don't mind being called malicious, but I do mind being called a fairy,' he growled.

Kurt Singer leaves a kinder picture of Keynes in action. He evoked 'by gesture, eye and word...the figure of a bird, of incredible swiftness, drawing circles in high altitudes but of deadly precision when suddenly sweeping down on some particular fact or thought, able to coin unforgettable word-formulas for what he saw, forcing his intellectual booty with iron grips even on the unwilling'.

It was not predetermined, either by background or abilities, that Keynes would make economics his life's work. His father was a logician and economist, but his career was not a good omen for his son: it ended in university administration. Keynes's mind was too wide-ranging, his spirit too active, for highly-specialized academic work. In writing his *Treatise on Probability*, he exhausted his serious interest in logic: it was too narrow for his mind. One must be able to use one's brains aesthetically and practically. The psychology of money, and stock-exchange gambling, fascinated him from an early age; his administrative talents might have made him a high imperial civil servant; he was a wonderful writer. In the end, he was able to use economics as the vehicle for all his obsessions and talents, but it was the uncertain state of a war-shocked world which made economics his vocation.

What sort of economist was Keynes? The most striking thing about him is the combination of gifts he brought to the subject. It is impossible to believe that he did not have himself in mind when he wrote, in his essay on Marshall,

the master-economist must possess a rare *combination* of
gifts ... He must be mathematician, historian, statesman,
philosopher – in some degree. He must understand symbols and
speak in words. He must contemplate the particular in terms of the
general, and touch abstract and concrete in the same flight of
thought. He must study the present in the light of the past for the
purposes of the future. No part of man's nature or his institutions
must lie entirely outside his regard. He must be purposeful and
disinterested in a simultaneous mood; as aloof and incorruptible as
an artist, yet sometimes as near the earth as a politician.

His wife, Lydia Lopokova, wrote that Keynes was 'more than
economist'; he himself felt that 'all his worlds' fertilized his
economic thinking. He fits that old-fashioned label, difficult to
define, of political economist, someone who sees economics as a
branch of statesmanship rather than a self-enclosed discipline with
invariable laws. One of his interlocutors on the Macmillan
Committee on Finance and Industry asked: had not social security
benefits prevented 'economic laws' from working? 'I do not think it
is any more economic law that wages should go down easily than
they should not,' Keynes replied. 'It is a question of facts. Economic
law does not lay down the facts: it tells you what the consequences
are.' In middle age, he used to complain bitterly that young
economists were not properly educated – they were not able to
draw on a wide culture for the interpretation of economic facts.
Here is a clue to what has gone wrong with economics, and indeed
with the Keynesian revolution. Keynes lit fires in technicians – but
they remained technicians. They used his tools, but failed to update
his vision.

In his essay on Thomas Malthus, Keynes claimed for 'the first
Cambridge economist', a 'profound economic intuition' and 'an
unusual combination of keeping an open mind to the shifting
picture of experience and of constantly applying to its
interpretation the principles of formal thought'. This expressed his
own philosophy of economics in a nutshell. Economics, he told Roy

Harrod in 1938, is 'a science of thinking in terms of models joined to the art of choosing models which are relevant to the contemporary world ... Good economists are scarce because the gift of using "vigilant observation" to choose good models ... appears to be a very rare one'. In his essay on Isaac Newton, Keynes quoted de Morgan's verdict of him: 'so happy in his conjectures as to seem to know more than he could possibly have any means of proving'. Keynes, too, felt sure of the result long before he had supplied the proof.

Keynes was the most intuitive of economists – using 'intuitive' as people talk, or used to talk, of 'feminine' intuition – a feeling of certainty apart from rationality. (One of his biographers, Charles Hession, traces his creativity to a synthesis of female intuition and masculine logic.) Intuition in this sense must be distinguished from philosophic intuition in which Keynes also believed – the view that knowledge arises directly from introspection. Keynes had an extraordinary insight into the *Gestalt* of particular situations. He had in marked degree the scientific imagination he ascribed to Freud, 'which can body forth an abundance of innovating ideas, shattering possibilities, working hypotheses, which have sufficient foundation in intuition and common experience'. His favoured objects of contemplation were economic facts, usually in statistical form. He used to say that his best ideas came to him from 'messing about with figures and *seeing* what they must mean'. Yet he was famously sceptical about econometrics – the use of statistical methods for forecasting purposes. He championed the cause of better statistics, not to provide material for the regression coefficient, but for the intuition of the economist to play on.

A crucial source of Keynes's understanding of business life was his personal involvement in money-making. 'It was his understanding of the speculative instinct which made Keynes such a great economist,' noted his friend and fellow financier Nicholas Davenport.

The academic economist never really knows what makes a businessman tick, why he wants sometimes to gamble on an investment project and why he sometimes prefers liquidity and cash. Maynard understood because he was a gambler himself and felt the gambling or liquidity instincts of the business man. He once said to me, 'Remember, Nicholas, that business life is always a bet.'

Keynes's generalizing passion was often at odds with his uncanny sense of the significant particular. He strove always 'To see a World in a Grain of Sand … And Eternity in an hour'. It was Keynes's very ability to 'touch the abstract and concrete in the same flight of thought' which is such a dazzling, but also bewildering, feature of his economics. People were never sure at what level of abstraction he was working. In his review of *The General Theory*, his Cambridge colleague Pigou complained of Keynes's desire to 'reach a stage of generality so high that everything must be discussed at the same time'. Schumpeter said much the same thing. *The General Theory* was a book which offered 'in the garb of general scientific truth, advice which … carries meaning only with reference to the practical exigencies of the unique historical situation of a given time and country'; it constructed 'special cases which in the author's own mind and in his exposition are invested with a treacherous generality'.

From another Cambridge colleague, Dennis Robertson, came a related criticism summed up in the phrase 'successive over-emphasis'.

> May I suggest that I – managing to keep throughout in touch with all the elements of the problem in a dim and fumbling way – have been a sort of glow worm, whose feeble glimmer lands on all the objects in the neighbourhood: while you, with your far more powerful intellect, have been a light-house casting a far more penetrating, but sometimes fatally distorting, beam on one object after another.

Marshall criticized Jevons in much the same way as many criticized Keynes: 'His success was aided even by his faults . . . he led many to think he was correcting great errors, whereas he was really only adding important explanations.'

There is obviously room to wonder whether, as Kurt Singer suggests, Keynes's 'general theory' is 'not in fact tailored to fit a very particular situation dominated by the political vicissitudes and their psychological consequences of that uneasy weekend between the two world wars; and whether [Keynes] was not in fact dealing with a phenomenon not likely to recur'. On the other hand, it is hard to explain the American collapse of 1929 in these terms; the extent of the 'uncaused' American depression, as we shall see, was the overwhelming fact which *The General Theory* was designed to explain.

In the final analysis, the shift from 'classical' to 'Keynesian' economics cannot be isolated from the larger transitions in politics, international affairs, science, philosophy, and aesthetics through which Keynes lived. They were all refracted in Keynes's luminous and mysterious mind. He remained an Edwardian, in the sense that his beliefs about the world were crystallized in the early years of the century. He adapted his creed to the grimmer realities which followed. In his economics, he strove not for the truth but for the attainable idea necessary to the conduct of lives in a world which had lost its moral bearings. He never succumbed to despair. In his darkest moments, cheerfulness kept breaking though. Shortly before his death, he gave a toast to economics and economists – 'trustees, not of civilisation, but of the possibilities of civilisation'. Only someone with a fine sense of language, and an Edwardian sense of life's purpose, would have chosen exactly those words.

Chapter 1
The life

Keynes set out to save what he called 'capitalistic individualism' from the scourge of mass unemployment, which, he saw, if left unchecked, would make 'authoritarian state systems' the norm in the Western world. He was born on 5 June 1883 into a very different era of 'capitalistic individualism': one in which economic progress was taken for granted; a liberal oligarchy of land and money manned the state; and Britain's position seemed secure as the head and heart of a world trading system. That this was an age which was dying was apparent only to a few. The doubts of the Victorians were still more religious than material, though there were premonitions of danger to the established order of things – the rise of the mass democracy at home, the challenge of Germany abroad, a certain loss of economic vitality, the growing amplitude of industrial fluctuations. The word 'unemployment' first appeared in the *Oxford English Dictionary* in 1888 – a sign of things to come.

Maynard Keynes was the product of a not unusual Victorian success story. He was the eldest of three children of a well-off Cambridge academic family, living at 6 Harvey Road. The Keynes family traced their descent back to a Norman knight who had come over with William the Conqueror. But it was Maynard Keynes's paternal grandfather who rescued the family from poverty by making a small fortune as a market gardener in Salisbury. His only son, John Neville, established himself at Cambridge in the 1870s as a Fellow of Pembroke College. He was a philosopher and an economist who wrote standard texts on logic and economic method; later he became Registrary of the University. In 1882, he married Florence Ada Brown, daughter of a well-known north-country Congregational minister, and a schoolmistress mother devoted to the cause of women's education. Both families' antecedents were 'chapel and trade': the move to Cambridge was part of the assimilation of provincial Nonconformity into the Establishment of Victorian England.

Keynes's parents embodied the Victorian virtues in relaxed form. John Neville Keynes indulged himself in a variety of hobbies. From him Maynard Keynes took intellectual precision and administrative efficiency combined with a certain playfulness, though he was mercifully free from his father's anxiety. Florence Keynes took up 'good causes' but never at the expense of her family. She – and the Browns generally – represented the 'preaching' and 'do-gooding' side of Maynard's inheritance; they also had a streak of intellectual fancy. Keynes's genius was his own, but he felt he had a social and intellectual tradition to live up to.

The family atmosphere at 6 Harvey Road was high-minded. The Keynes circle included some of the foremost economists and philosophers of the day – Alfred Marshall, Herbert Foxwell, Henry Sidgwick, W. E. Johnston, James Ward. As a young man Maynard played golf with Sidgwick, and wrote of him with wicked accuracy (to his friend Bernard Swithinbank on 27 March 1906): 'He never did anything but wonder whether Christianity was true and prove that it wasn't and hope that it was.' Cambridge was less worldly than Oxford. Although Maynard would mingle with the world, his standards remained unworldly. He judged his own life, and others', by intellectual and aesthetic criteria. He imposed himself on the world of affairs by force of intellect and imagination, but was not absorbed by it.

He accepted without question the high value his father and mother placed on academic excellence. Indeed, he never rebelled against his parents, though he had a larger range of sympathies. His family home, where Neville and Florence Keynes continued to live after Maynard had died, gave his life stability and continuity. His social thinking had a precise reference to his family's circumstances. He saw himself as a member of the 'thinking' middle class. He thought that escape from poverty was always possible in pre-war Europe 'for any man of capacity or character at all exceeding the average'. And he never lost his belief in the duty of a capable and right-thinking clerisy to give leadership to the masses.

In 1897, he gained a scholarship to Eton, Britain's top school. He was an outstanding schoolboy, though in no narrow way, winning an enormous number of prizes, being elected to 'Pop', Eton's exclusive social club, and even performing creditably in the College's incomprehensible Wall game. What is already noticeable is the extraordinary range of his interests and aptitudes. Mathematics was his best subject, but he excelled in classics and history too. He got through his work at lightning speed. He won the respect of scholars *and* athletes, just as later he would win over both academic economists and practical men. Keynes realized from an early age that cleverness guilefully deployed was the road to success in dealing with adults. Cleverness was the alternative to submission or rebellion: through cleverness one could manipulate any situation to one's advantage. What was also noticeable was a certain mismatch between his capacities and his sympathies. He was developing into the logical, statistical, administrative, arrogant Keynes; but he was also the 'Maynard' whom his intimate friends knew, craving affection, drawn to writers, artists, and dreamers, losing himself in medieval poetry or abstruse speculations. Later he would see the practical purpose of economics as providing a protective belt for civilization against the forces of madness and ignorance.

In 1902, he went up to King's College, Cambridge, on an open scholarship in mathematics and classics. Mathematics, his best subject, had never given him much pleasure, and he gave it up with relief after gaining a first-class degree in Part I of the Mathematical Tripos. He had spent most of his undergraduate time doing other things – studying philosophy, writing a paper on the medieval logician Peter Abelard, speaking at the Cambridge Union (he became its president in 1905), playing bridge, and indulging his passion for friendship. In 1906, he came second to Otto Niemeyer in the Civil Service Examination, entering the India Office as a junior clerk. In two years of routine work, he picked up a sound knowledge of India's financial system, which led to his appointment as a member of the Royal Commission on Indian Finance and Currency in 1913. But he spent most of his office hours writing a dissertation on probability which, after one failure, got him his fellowship at King's College in 1909. Cambridge University remained his academic home for the rest of his life.

While he was thus laying the foundations of his career, a shift in values had been taking place which carried him far beyond the confines of his parents' relaxed Victorianism. Victorian morals had been sustained by religious beliefs which were collapsing. Keynes and his undergraduate friends were militant atheists; but, as with so many thinking Nonconformists, the loss of beliefs which they regarded as false had not removed the need for beliefs which they could regard as true. They looked to moral philosophy to tell them how to live their lives. The philosopher G. E. Moore gave them what they wanted – a justification for breaking with the social and sexual codes of their parents. His *Principia Ethica* (1903) was the manifesto of modernism to Keynes's generation: later Keynes described it as 'the opening of a new heaven on earth'.

Keynes had fallen under Moore's influence when, in his second undergraduate term, he was elected a member of the Cambridge Apostles, a selective and (at the time) secret philosophical discussion society. Through the Apostles he made some of the great

17

friendships of his life, notably with Lytton Strachey; in the late 1900s he became a member of the Bloomsbury Group, a London commune of Apostles, their friends, and male and female relations. It was a circle of young writers and artists who found in the freer life of the unfashionable Bloomsbury district of London an escape from the stuffy conventions of their parents' households. In this partly admiring, partly disapproving, frequently malicious group of talented friends, Maynard Keynes found his emotional home before his marriage.

Moore convinced them of the supreme value of aesthetic experiences and personal friendship. He swept away the melancholy of the previous generation who could find no convincing reasons for doing their duty. He reintroduced cheerfulness into moral discussion, erecting a new argument for unworldliness on the foundation of Cambridge analytical philosophy. It was a shift possible only for those in privileged circumstances, and for whom politics was a minor interest, lacking the power to disturb 'good states of mind' – something certainly true of Keynes before 1914. But it was immensely liberating.

'One's prime objects in life', wrote Keynes in 1938 of his pre-war days, 'were love, the creation and enjoyment of aesthetic experience and the pursuit of knowledge. Of these love came a long way first'. To Keynes and most of his Apostolic friends, love meant homosexual love, initially of a somewhat spiritualized kind. Keynes's lover from 1908 to 1911 was the painter Duncan Grant, a cousin of Lytton Strachey, whom he 'stole' from the latter to much perturbation in Bloomsbury. Until after the First World War all his emotional attachments were to young men. But Keynes was no more an extremist in love than in economics or politics. His homosexuality did not exclude the capacity to fall in love, and enjoy a happy sexual relationship, with the right woman; and she duly appeared after the First World War.

Beauty for Keynes and his friends meant chiefly Post-Impressionist painting, Russian ballet, and the new styles of decorative art influenced by both. For those with money, taste, and domestic servants (and one did not have to have much money to afford servants), London just before the First World War was an exciting place. The British philistinism of which Matthew Arnold had complained was being undermined by the artistic *avant-garde*. The idea that preposterous figures in Central Europe might be able to close down civilization in pursuit of great power ambitions and ethnic rivalries seemed unthinkable. It was a world, also, completely cut off from the ordinary experience of the masses, for whom, nevertheless, automatic economic progress was believed to be producing a better life, too.

Pursuit of knowledge for Keynes meant philosophy and economics, and more the first than the second. Most of his intellectual energy before 1914 went into turning his dissertation into the *Treatise on Probability*, not published till 1921, in which he tried to widen the field of logical argument to cover those cases where conclusions were uncertain. This work spilled over importantly into his economics. At Cambridge he lectured on money. He was an orthodox Marshallian quantity theorist, and did little to extend the frontiers of the subject, though his first (and only pre-war) book, *Indian Currency and Finance* (1913), was a lucid attempt to apply existing monetary theory to the reform of India's currency system. It was notable for its expert knowledge of the working of financial institutions, its endorsement of the gold-exchange standard, and its advocacy of an Indian central bank – details of which Keynes worked out as a member of the Royal Commission on Indian Finance and Currency the same year.

He was just as interested, though, in the problem of knowledge in economics, engaging, in 1911, in an acrimonious debate with Karl Pearson about the influence of the alcoholism of parents on the life chances of their children. Keynes rejected Pearson's use of inductive methods to establish social truths. This reflected his more general scepticism about the value of statistical inference, in line with his rejection of the statistical, or frequency, theory of probability. Economics could not be an exact science, because the number of variables was too great, and stability of variables over time could not be guaranteed. As he was to put it later, it is better to be roughly right than precisely wrong.

Keynes was 31 when the First World War broke out. The war changed his life-style, career, and ambitions, though not his ultimate values. After playing an important part in averting the collapse of the gold standard in the banking crisis of August 1914, he joined the Treasury in January 1915, remaining there till his resignation in June 1919. In January 1917, he became head of a new 'A' division, managing Britain's external finance. Over the period he helped build up the system of Allied purchases in external markets, which were being largely financed by Britain. He proved, in fact, to be a great Treasury official, adapting naturally to Whitehall, endlessly fertile in applying basic principles to concrete situations, able to turn out, at lightning speed, short, lucid memoranda, so invaluable to overworked ministers. Whitehall also satisfied that part of his nature which craved for mastery over the material world. He enjoyed his work and delighted in the company of the great and powerful which his position as a Treasury mandarin, brilliant, personable, single, good at bridge, full of amusing gossip, gave him.

Yet this, the face displayed by Sir Roy Harrod in his official biography, was a mask which hid a profound inner conflict. Keynes and his circle had been shocked by the outbreak of the war, which extinguished their hopes for a 'new civilization'. As it progressed, they came to believe in it less and less. Keynes played his part in the war effort to growing criticism from his Bloomsbury and pacifist friends, and with growing unease of conscience. He justified his position in a number of ways. From the summer of 1915 to January 1916, he provided the chancellor of the exchequer, Reginald McKenna, with economic arguments against conscription. His case, set out in powerful memoranda, was that Britain should concentrate on subsidizing its Allies by earning foreign exchange, rather than squandering men and munitions on the Western Front. This was a rational argument, based on the principle of the division of labour. But underlying it was a growing hatred of the war, and a desire to keep it away from his friends. It also earned him the hostility of Lloyd George, who believed in the 'knockout blow'.

When conscription came in January 1916, Keynes wanted McKenna, Runciman, and other leaders of Asquithian liberalism to quit the government, and proposed to go into opposition with them. When they stayed on, he stayed on too, but not before he had applied for exemption from the Military Service Act as a conscientious objector – a symbolic gesture, as he was automatically exempted by his Treasury work. Over the next six months he used his official position to help Duncan Grant and others get exemption from military service by testifying, as he put it, 'to the sincerity, virtue and truthfulness of my friends'. Keynes and his circle were not pacifists on principle, but they were liberals who held that the state had no right to make people fight. They had also come to believe that this war was not worth fighting, and that every effort should be made to end it by a compromise peace. In December 1916, Lloyd George became prime minister, in the midst of a financial crisis which threatened to deprive Britain of the means of paying for any more war purchases in the United States. Keynes wrote to Duncan Grant on 14 January 1917: 'God curse him [Lloyd George] . . . I pray for the most absolute financial crash and yet strive to prevent it – so that all I do is a contradiction to all I feel.'

Keynes's growing hostility to the war was influenced by the fact that it was making Britain dependent on the United States. With the depletion of its own assets it needed to borrow from America to supply its own Allies, especially Russia. On 24 October 1916, above the initials of Reginald McKenna, chancellor of the exchequer, appeared the words, almost certainly drafted by Keynes: 'If things go on as at present ... the President of the American Republic will be in a position ... to dictate his own terms to us.' This fixes the moment when financial hegemony passed across the Atlantic. The same story was to be repeated in the Second World War. Consciousness of Britain's (and Europe's) decline relative to that of the United States gave an added urgency to Keynes's quest for a negotiated peace; it shaped much of his post-war thinking.

In September 1917, Keynes went to Washington for the first of his loan negotiations, and did not like the experience. 'The only really sympathetic and original thing in America is the niggers, who are charming,' he wrote to Duncan Grant. He was not a success with the Americans either, making 'a terrible impression for his rudeness out here', according to Basil Blackett, a Treasury colleague at the British Embassy. It was the start of a troubled relationship which lasted till Keynes died.

By the end of 1917, Keynes was convinced, as he told his mother, that the continuation of the war would mean 'the disappearance of the social order we have known hitherto ... What frightens me is the prospect of *general impoverishment*. In another year's time, we shall have forfeited the claim we have staked out in the New World and in exchange this country will be mortgaged to America.' This summarizes the mood which dominates his *Economic Consequences of the Peace*, his elegy on a vanished age and polemic against the Treaty of Versailles, published in December 1919. By that time, Russia had succumbed to Bolshevism, revolution had broken out in Germany and Hungary, inflation was rampant, much of Europe was starving. Yet all the peacemakers could think about was 'frontiers and sovereignties'. As chief Treasury representative at the Paris Peace Conference, Keynes had tried hard to get Lloyd George to agree to a moderate figure for German reparations. When he failed, he resigned in disgust on 7 June 1919. He wrote his book in the summer of 1919 at Charleston, the Sussex home of Vanessa Bell and Duncan Grant.

The Economic Consequences of the Peace denounced the folly of the peacemakers in trying to extort from Germany an indemnity it could not possibly pay. He foresaw that attempts to make it pay would destroy the economic mechanisms on which the pre-war prosperity of Continental Europe had depended. He predicted a war of vengeance by Germany. There were memorable portraits of the leading peacemakers, Georges Clemenceau and Woodrow Wilson, though he left out the sketch of Lloyd George on Asquith's advice.

Keynes's main proposals were to cancel all inter-Ally war debts; limit Germany's liability for reparation to a modest annual sum, payable to France and Belgium; and restore Germany as the economic powerhouse of the Continent – Russia would be rebuilt 'through the agency of German enterprise and organisation'. The cancellation of inter-Ally war debts was designed to de-couple American finance from Europe. Keynes supported American loans to get European industry restarted, pay for essential food imports, and stabilize currencies. But he was adamantly opposed to Europeans borrowing from the United States to service deadweight debt.

His book became an international best-seller, had a profound effect on post-war thinking, and made Keynes world-famous. It would be far too simple to say it *created* the mood of appeasement of Germany: revulsion against wartime propaganda had already started. What it did was to turn attention from Great Power politics to the conditions of economic prosperity. Keynes put economics on the map for the informed general public, and it has been there ever since. The view that capitalism needed managing also started to sink in. Keynes did not emerge from the war a socialist, much less a Bolshevik. Socialism, he started to say, was for later – after the economic problem had been solved: a curious link with classical Marxism. He remained a Liberal till he died. The task he set himself was to reconstruct the capitalist social order on the basis of improved technical management.

The war also brought about a rearrangement in his personal life, which finally shed the undergraduate flavour which had persisted till 1914. He was now a great man, a world authority on international finance, whose writings caused currencies to tremble, whose counsel was sought by financiers, politicians, and public officials in all countries. He returned to Cambridge in October 1919, but Cambridge was no longer the centre of his life. He was resident only in term-time, and even then only for long weekends (usually Thursday evenings to Tuesday mornings) into which he packed his much-reduced teaching duties, his College committees, and a social life which revolved round his family at 6 Harvey Road and a few close friends among the younger dons. Between the wars he was the spectacularly successful investment bursar of King's College, boosting the capital of the college 'Chest' from £30,000 in 1920 to over £300,000 by 1945.

His London base was 46 Gordon Square, the Bloomsbury Group's *monument historique*. Here he spent mid-weeks in term-time, and the first part of each vacation. London life was even more packed with activity. At various times he was on the boards of no less than five investment and insurance companies, the chief one being the National Mutual Life Assurance Company, whose chairman he was from 1921 to 1937. From 1923 to 1931, he was chief proprietor and chairman of the board of the weekly journal, the *Nation and Atheneum*, working closely with its editor, Hubert Henderson. His editorship of the *Economic Journal* (1911–37) was also conducted from London. London was crucial to Keynes as a base of influence. He had direct access, for much of the interwar years, to prime ministers and chancellors. In the 1920s, his evolving ideas on economic policy permeated the official mind through monthly meetings of the Tuesday Club, a dining club of bankers, Treasury officials, economists, and financial journalists started by the stock-broker Oswald Falk in 1917; in the 1930s he sought to influence policy through his membership of the prime minister's Economic Advisory Council.

In the 1920s, Oswald Falk was Keynes's main partner in moneymaking. They started speculating on currencies immediately after the war, and continued in commodities. Despite three major reverses – in 1920, 1928–9, and 1937–8 – Keynes increased his net assets from £16,315 in 1919 to £411,238 – £10m in today's values – by the time he died. Over the interwar years, his investment philosophy shifted from currency and commodity speculation to investment in blue-chip companies in line with his changing economic theory. The failure of his 'credit cycle' investment theory to make him money led him to the 'animal spirits' theory of investment behaviour of *The General Theory*, and to a personal investment philosophy of 'faithfulness'. (To counter investment volatility he urged that the relationship between an investor and his share should be like that of husband and wife.) Journalism was another major source of money-making, especially in the early 1920s. Three major coups between 1921 and 1922, plus other journalistic earnings, netted him today's equivalent of £100,000. His successes in money-making in turn financed his activities as a collector of pictures and rare books, in homage to his youthful ideal of the good life.

The most dramatic sign of the reorganization of his life was his marriage. He first met the ballerina Lydia Lopokova in October 1918, when the Diaghilev ballet returned to London; he started wooing her at the end of 1921 when she danced in Diaghilev's magnificent, but commercially unsuccessful, production of Tchaikovsky's *Sleeping Beauty* at the Alhambra theatre. Diminutive and pert, with a turned-up nose, and a head which reminded Virginia Woolf of a plover's egg, Lydia was an outstanding artist in her own right, with a bawdy sense of humour, a genius for refashioning the English language (she once referred to 'Jesus fomenting water into wine at Cannes'), and strong and secure intuitions, directly expressed. Keynes was captivated by her, and they were married on 4 August 1925. Possibly only a woman as exotic as Lydia, and coming from right outside his own social milieu, could have won the heart of a man whose affections were basically directed towards his own sex. Despite much Bloomsbury foreboding, she proved a perfect wife for him. She gave his life the emotional stability it had lacked for many years, and which provided the necessary background to sustained intellectual effort. In 1925, he acquired the lease of Tilton, a farmhouse in East Sussex, close to Charleston. Here he and Lydia passed his vacations, with friends and relations coming to stay; in a rather damp annexe to the main house he wrote most of his two major theoretical works, *A Treatise on Money* and *The General Theory of Employment, Interest, and Money*.

Keynes had always been a busy man. In the interwar years, his activity spilt out in masses of new directions. Contemporaries knew him as the man with the bulging brief-case, hurrying from one place, one meeting, to another. His life was embedded in a dense mass of miscellaneous activities which both fertilized and distracted him from his writing. His failure to produce a major work of theory till 1930, when he was almost 50, was the price he paid. But perhaps it was just as well, in the 1920s, to keep one's intellectual investments reasonably liquid. Economic theory was in a state of flux. It took the interwar 'shocks' to the capitalist system to crystallize the indictment of old-fashioned understandings of economic behaviour. Keynes's growing fame and involvement in public affairs also narrowed the circle, and quality, of his friendships. Outside his marriage, there was less time for 'personal moments'. 'Doing good' took precedence over 'being good'. But he never renounced the ideals of his youth; and though he was always busy, the speed and efficiency with which he got through his work gave the impression of unhurried calm.

The spur to Keynes's theoretical and practical efforts between the wars was his fear for the future. The pre-war mood of sexual and cultural freedom, made possible by the expectation of 'automatic' progress, had given way to a sense of the extraordinary precariousness of capitalist civilization. This was reinforced by the catastrophes of the interwar years – especially the Great

Depression of 1929–33 and the triumph of Hitler in Germany. Belief in the stability and resilience of the market system was replaced by the view that the 19th-century era of *laissez-faire* was a unique episode in economic history, dependent on special conjunctures which were no more; that, despite technical progress, mankind was in danger of retrogressing from the plateau of prosperity and civilization it had achieved in the Victorian age. One way of interpreting Keynes's forebodings is to see them as a delayed reaction to the 19th-century fear of life without God. In 1925, after a visit to Soviet Russia, Keynes wrote that 'modern capitalism is absolutely irreligious ... Such a system has to be immensely, not merely moderately, successful to survive.' This was the spiritual and psychological background to the Keynesian 'mood'.

In the years immediately following the war, Keynes's attention focused on two things: the international financial disorganization which the war had brought about, and which the peacemaking at Versailles had worsened, and the deterioration in the equilibrium terms of trade between Europe and the New World. At existing productivity levels, Europeans would have to accept a lower standard of life than before the war, since a given quantity of manufactured exports was buying less food and raw materials from abroad than hitherto. This range of concerns can be followed in Keynes's contributions to the *Manchester Guardian Commercial*'s Reconstruction Supplements, the twelve issues of which he edited between 1922 and 1923. The 'neo-Malthusian' strand in Keynes's thinking has not been sufficiently noticed. It was at the heart of his argument for a devaluation of the main European currencies against the dollar.

Despite his resignation from the Treasury, and the odium which *Economic Consequences of the Peace* had aroused in some 'official circles', Keynes played a far from negligible role in sorting out the mess left by the peacemakers. He contributed directly to the British Treasury plan for settling the reparation problem at the end of

1922; and, through his friendship with the Hamburg banker Carl Melchior, acted almost as unofficial adviser to the German government in 1922–3, a curiously under-researched role.

Until 1923, Keynes was not specially concerned with British problems, which seemed trivial in comparison with those of the Continent. However, the emergence of persisting mass unemployment turned his attention to this unique feature of the British situation. He attributed the bulk of the abnormal British unemployment of the 1920s to monetary mismanagement. Refusal to raise bank rate soon or high enough had allowed the inflationary boom of 1919–20 to get out of hand; the maintenance of punitive real rates of interest right through the subsequent period of falling prices, output, and employment had made the depression far deeper than it need have been. Keynes attributed the second phase of policy to the desire not just to eliminate the post-war inflation (which he shared), but to lower the price level sufficiently to put the pound back on the gold standard at its pre-war parity with the dollar: £1 = $4.86. Like all economists, Keynes expected British employment to recover to 'normal' (as measured by pre-war standards) when prices 'settled down' in 1922. But unemployment remained obstinately stuck at above 10%. It was its failure to come down much below this rate for the rest of the 1920s which alerted Keynes to the possibility that the employment costs of a savage deflation might be more than 'transitional', with the economy remaining 'jammed' in a low-employment trap. To explain how such an 'underemployment equilibrium' could occur would be the main object of his theoretical writing.

A Tract on Monetary Reform (1923) was an attempt to design what would now be called a monetary 'regime' which would allow reasonable steadiness of economic activity. Keynes rejected the gold standard as the appropriate regime. The requirement that domestic currency should be convertible into gold at a fixed official price did not guarantee the stable domestic price level which Keynes considered essential for stable business expectations, because the value of gold itself was liable to fluctuate in terms of goods, depending on its scarcity or plenty. Further, given the actual and prospective distribution of the world's gold reserves, returning to the gold standard would be to surrender Britain's control over its own price level to the Federal Reserve Board in Washington. Britain should remain free to manage its exchange rate in accordance with the needs of its domestic economy. Such a system of domestic monetary control would, Keynes argued, be consistent with short-run exchange-rate stability. But exchange-rate stability would be a consequence of stable domestic prices, not an independent, much less overriding, objective of policy.

A Tract on Monetary Reform identified Keynes as the foremost intellectual opponent of the 'official' policy of returning sterling to the gold standard at the pre-war parity with the dollar. But his plea for a 'managed' currency found little favour. Winston Churchill, the chancellor of the exchequer, put sterling back on the gold standard at \$4.86 on 20 April 1925. Keynes immediately attacked the decision in a memorable pamphlet, *The Economic Consequences of Mr. Churchill*. He argued that the revaluation of sterling required a 10% reduction in British wage costs, which could be achieved only by 'intensifying unemployment without limit'. Implicit in this argument was the notion that the cost of labour was the main influence on the price level: under modern conditions of trade-union-led wage bargaining, a reduction in the quantity of money led directly to a reduction in the quantity of employment. He predicted that actual monetary policy would shrink from the attempt to restore equilibrium by this method. Interest rates would be kept high enough to attract foreign funds to London; but not pushed so high as to break trade-union resistance to a reduction in the money-wage per worker employed. The result would be a low-employment economy. So it proved. Despite the defeat of the General Strike in 1926, employers made little effort to reduce money-wages, which remained steady for the rest of the 1920s although the price level sagged. Keynes was the first to realize and state clearly that an overvalued currency would be a weak, not a strong, currency.

The events surrounding the General Strike shifted Keynes's political allegiance from Asquith to Lloyd George, as well as bringing about a greater sympathy for the Labour Party. Between 1926 and 1929, he played a notable part in shaping the policy of the Lloyd George Liberal Party. Lloyd George looked to Keynes to provide the economic programme which would win the Liberals at least a share of power; Keynes saw Lloyd George as the most promising instrument for 'conquering unemployment'. Keynes's service on the Liberal Industrial Inquiry in 1927–8 marked the high point in his involvement in politics. It was also the one period of his life when he thought deeply about the structural problems of British industry. The product of this phase was his political philosophy of the Middle Way, first outlined in his pamphlet *The End of Laissez-Faire* (1926).

Keynes spent the years 1925–8 partly writing his *Treatise on Money*, which started as a development of the ideas of the *Tract*. His main intellectual companion at this time was Dennis Robertson, Fellow of Trinity College, a retiring man, but tenacious controversialist. Keynes had no disciples in the mid-1920s: Kurt Singer remembers him as 'a lonely figure, pathetic, rebellious and fond of dominating; but not yet in possession of the watchword that establishes leadership'. But a younger generation of those who helped make the Keynesian Revolution were starting to take root in Cambridge: the Italian *émigré* Piero Sraffa; Joan and Austin Robinson; above all Richard Kahn, whom Keynes described as his 'favourite pupil'. Keynes struck one of his students, H. M. Robertson, as 'more like a stockbroker than a don', with his City suits and City gossip.

A Treatise on Money, published in 1930, is an excellent example of Keynes's passion for generalization. In essence, Keynes built an exceedingly complicated conceptual apparatus to show how an economy on the gold standard could, under certain conditions, fall into a low-employment trap. If the monetary authority was prevented from lowering the long-term interest rate to a level consonant with investors' expectations, and if domestic costs of production prevented the achievement of an export surplus equal to what people wished to lend abroad, the result would be an 'excess' of saving over investment, a sagging price level, and a 'jammed' economy. This was Britain's fate in the 1920s. The revolutionary thought, brought out more clearly in *The General Theory*, was that there was no automatic mechanism in a modern economic system to keep intended saving in equilibrium with intended investment. As Hayek alone discerned, this was equivalent to saying that there was no automatic mechanism in the system to adjust aggregate demand to supply. It was in the notion of domestic savings unmatched by domestic or foreign investment that Keynes found his rationale for a programme of loan-financed public works to increase employment within the constraints of the gold-standard system.

Keynes's public endorsement, in April 1929, of the Lloyd George policy of loan-financed public works, in *Can Lloyd George do it?*, written jointly with Hubert Henderson, was notable for the argument that spending on public works would produce a 'cumulative' wave of prosperity. His chance to influence the policy of Ramsay MacDonald's second Labour government came with his appointment to the Macmillan Committee on Finance and Industry set up in November 1929, and to the government's Economic Advisory Council, established in January 1930. His nine-day exposition of the theory of the *Treatise* and possible remedies for unemployment to the Macmillan Committee in March 1930 marks the real start of the Keynesian revolution in economic policy. But his proposals for public works and protection made little headway at the time. The collapse of the world economy and business confidence strengthened the forces of orthodoxy. The pressure for retrenchment in the public finances brought about the replacement of the Labour government by a National government on 25 August 1931. On 21 September, the financial collapse in Central Europe, together with a burgeoning British current account deficit, forced sterling off the gold standard. That autumn Keynes set out to write a new book of theory designed to emphasize the role of output changes in the adjustment to a new position of equilibrium.

Although Keynes wrote one policy pamphlet, *The Means to Prosperity*, in 1933, the bulk of his 'spare time' between 1931 and 1935 was spent not advising governments, but writing his *General Theory of Employment, Interest, and Money*, published in February 1936. Two books of essays also appeared – *Essays in Persuasion* (1931) and *Essays in Biography* (1933). The first collected what Keynes, in his introduction, called 'the croakings of twelve years – the croakings of a Cassandra who could never influence the course of events in time'. A notable feature of the second is Keynes's use of short lives of men of science to ponder and delineate the character of scientific genius.

In the period 1931–2, Keynes engaged in intermittent, but intense, correspondence on points of theory with Hawtrey, Robertson, and Hayek. He was also helped by a 'Cambridge Circus' of young economists, the chief of whom, Richard Kahn, supplied him with the theory of the multiplier. Evidence of the progress of the book is given not only by *The Means to Prosperity*, but by early drafts of chapters, fragments of lectures, and a complete set of lecture notes taken by some of Keynes's students from 1932 to 1935. One of them, A. C. Gilpin, described the Cambridge atmosphere in 1933 in a letter to his parents:

> Economics lectures this year seem mainly to insist of elaborations or refutations of theories taught us last year. Shove dissects Marshall; Keynes attacks Pigou; Robertson disagrees with Keynes, and leaves it to his audience to decide who is right; an intense lady, Mrs. Joan Robinson, tries to explain why they disagree. It is interesting but confusing.

At the final proof stage in the summer of 1935, Roy Harrod made important suggestions.

Keynes was never a person to be doing one thing at a time. In addition to work on the book, he spent much of 1934–5 planning and supervising the building of the Cambridge Arts theatre, in fulfilment of a pre-war dream of endowing Cambridge with a permanent centre for the dramatic arts. As bursar of King's College, Cambridge, and as 'squire of Tilton', he became involved in ever more extensive farming operations. These are reflected in two articles he wrote in 1933 in praise of 'National Self-Sufficieny', which combined a moral attack on the international division of labour with the argument that 'most modern mass-production processes can be performed in most countries and climates with almost equal efficiency'. There were two visits to the United States, in 1931 and 1934. On the second, Keynes met Roosevelt, and most of the architects, as well as some of the critics, of the 'New Deal'. The influence of his presence and writing on the first phase of the 'New Deal' has been underestimated.

The General Theory changed the way most economists understood the working of economies. In that sense, it was explicitly, and successfully, revolutionary. It also had a revolutionary effect on policy. Not immediately, but after the Second World War, Western governments openly or implicitly committed themselves to maintaining a high level of employment. *The General Theory* itself is a profound exploration of the logic of economic behaviour under uncertainty, combined with a short-period model of income determination, which emphasized quantity, rather than price, adjustment. These two loosely linked strands gave rise to much subsequent dispute concerning the 'real meaning' of *The General Theory* between what Alan Coddington called the 'fundamentalist' and the 'hydraulic' Keynesians. It was the income-determination model, based on the multiplier, together with the consequent development of national income statistics, which made Keynesian economics acceptable to policy-makers, since it offered them a seemingly secure method of forecasting and controlling the movement of such 'real' variables as investment, consumption, and employment.

Keynes's own first attempt to apply *The General Theory* to policy came in three articles he wrote for *The Times* in January 1937 on 'How to Avoid a Slump' – a notably cautious assessment of the possibility of reducing unemployment below its then current rate of 12% by injecting 'greater aggregate demand' into the economy. Keynes had never enjoyed robust health. In May 1937, at the age of 53, he suffered a coronary thrombosis, from which he recovered only slowly. By the time war broke out, on 3 September 1939, a Hungarian physician, János Plesch, had restored him to something like his old vigour.

Following the publication of *The General Theory*, Keynes became the most influential figure in British economic policy. He achieved this by force of mind and personality, rather than by political position. Despite many offers, he never stood for Parliament. In June 1940, he was made a member of a Consultative Committee set up to advise the chancellor of the exchequer on war problems; in August he received a room at the Treasury and a part-time secretary. He had 'no routine duties and no office hours ... but a sort of roving commission plus membership of many high up committees, which allow me to butt in in almost any direction where I think I have something to say'. Keynes used his anomalous position to intervene, often decisively, on the whole range of economic business, great and small. He became the most powerful civil servant at large Whitehall has ever had, 'less the servant and more the master of those he served'. His elevation to the peerage in 1942, as Baron Keynes of Tilton, would have given him the opportunity to enter the government, but this was never suggested, probably because he was too useful where he was. It did, however, give him the rank to represent the government on several important missions to the United States, his last as joint head (with Lord Halifax) of the British delegation to Washington in September 1945 to negotiate the American loan.

Keynes's most important service in the last period of his life was to help build the domestic and international foundations of the managed capitalism to which his theory pointed. Three of his contributions to post-war statesmanship deserve particular mention.

The first arose in the context of wartime finance. One possible implication of Keynesian theory is that the government's budget should be used to balance the accounts of the nation, not just the government, to ensure that aggregate supply and demand are equal at full employment. In wartime, the problem was not to achieve full employment – which was reached in 1940 – but to prevent inflation – total demand rising higher than total supply. The specific task of wartime finance was to make sure that the extra demand created by full employment was spent by the government not by the private consumer. In three articles to *The Times*, published in October 1939, and reproduced as a pamphlet, *How to Pay for the War*, Keynes put forward a scheme for compulsory saving or 'deferred pay', in which excess purchasing power would be mopped up by a progressive surcharge on all incomes (with offsets to the poor in the form of family allowances), part of which would be given back in instalments after the war in order to counteract the anticipated post-war slump. Although this scheme was adopted only in part, Keynes's analytical approach, together with the estimates of national income which he used to calculate the size of the 'inflationary gap', became the basis of the budgetary strategy for the whole war, starting with Kingsley Wood's budget in 1941. But its importance went beyond that. In 1939, Keynes had doubted whether 'capitalistic democracy' would ever be willing to make the 'grand experiment' which would prove his theory. In war the experiment was made, and the theory worked. The economy was run at full capacity with only very moderate inflation. What could be done in war could be done in peace – or so it seemed.

Keynes's second major contribution to the post-war order was his part in establishing the Bretton Woods system. This was unfinished business left over from the collapse of the old order. Even in his *Tract* period Keynes was not a currency floater. He wanted a 'managed' exchange-rate system – something consistent with *de facto* stability of exchange rates for long periods.

His famous Clearing Union plan of 1942 provided for a link between each national currency and a new reserve asset 'bancor'. Surplus countries would accumulate 'bancor' balances in the Union's Clearing Bank; overdraft facilities would be made available to deficit countries up to the total of the surpluses. The scheme was designed to discourage countries from running persistent balance of payments surpluses. If they nevertheless did so, debtors could automatically draw on the creditors' bancor balances. Despite the defeat of this plan by Harry Dexter White's alternative scheme for a gold-exchange standard backed by a small 'adjustment' facility (the International Monetary Fund), Keynes none the less worked unsparingly to achieve the Bretton Woods Agreement and to ensure support for it in Britain, taking part in two exhaustive negotiations in Washington in 1943 and 1944. In doing so, he played a decisive part in bringing Britain (and Europe) down on the liberal side of the shape of the post-war international economic order.

Keynes's third act of statesmanship was to negotiate the American loan in September–December 1945. He estimated that Britain's deficit on current account would total nearly $7bn over the first three post-war years. Keynes went to Washington in September 1945 to seek a grant of $5bn 'without strings'. He returned, three months and several famous rows later, with a loan of $3.75bn conditional on a commitment to make sterling convertible into other currencies a year after the loan agreement was ratified. It was probably the most humiliating experience of his life. For somone who had started as one of the rulers of a world empire to have to go begging to the United States was a bitter pill. Yet Keynes swallowed it, and persuaded the new Labour government to swallow it, because, as he put it to Lord Halifax, the alternative was 'Nazi or Communist' methods. In the House of Lords, he made an eloquent speech in defence of the agreement.

Keynes never recovered properly from the strain of the loan negotiations. There was another trip to the United States, to Savannah in March 1946, to inaugurate the International Monetary Fund. Once again, Keynes was involved in a quarrel with the Americans over the question of the Fund's management. As always he pursued other business as well. During the war, he had added to his Treasury duties the chairmanship of CEMA – the Council for the Encouragement of Music and the Arts. In 1945, he was appointed first chairman of the Arts Council. Stopping over in New York after the Savannah meeting, he arranged for the American ballet to come over to Covent Garden, whose gala reopening performance of *Sleeping Beauty* he had attended on 20 February 1946. Two months later, on 21 April 1946, he was dead, of a massive coronary thrombosis. There was an imposing memorial service at Westminster Abbey, but he had chosen his own epitaph many years earlier, as an Eton schoolboy, when he quoted a passage from Bernard of Cluny's *De Contemptu Mundi*:

> Not only those
> Who hold clear echoes of the voice divine
> Are honourable – they are blest, indeed,
> Whate'er the world has held – but those who hear
> Some fair faint echoes, though the crowd be deaf,
> And see the white gods' garments on the hills,
> Which the crowd sees not, though they may not find
> Fit music for their visions, they are blest,
> Not pitiable.

Chapter 2
Keynes's philosophy of practice

Keynes's economics – unlike Keynesian economics – was philosophically driven. It was informed by his vision of the 'good life'; it was permeated by his theory of probability. These philosophical foundations were laid early in his life. Philosophy came before economics; and the philosophy of ends came before the philosophy of means.

Keynes's philosophy was the product of an atheistic generation. He and his contemporaries saw themselves as replacing Christian 'hocus-pocus' by a rational system of ethics and conduct. But they used tools of thought inherited from the Christian (as well as Greek) past; and the structure of their thought was metaphysical.

Fundamental was Keynes's intuitionist epistemology. He regarded intuition, rather than sense experience, as the foundation of knowledge, including ethical knowledge – a tradition going back to Plato. His stress on intuitive reasoning in economics, as well as his hostility to econometrics, was thus philosophically based, and not just temperamental.

His ethical beliefs were derived from G. E. Moore's *Principia Ethica*, published in 1903, his second undergraduate year. 'I see no reason to shift from the fundamental intuitions of *Principia Ethica*', Keynes said in 1938. Three things he got from Moore seem particularly important. The first was the indefinability of good. Good, Moore said, is the name of a simple, non-natural property, intuitively known. Secondly, good and bad states of mind are prior to good and bad actions: value determines duty. Finally, 'By far the most valuable things which we know or can imagine, are certain states of consciousness, which may be roughly described as the pleasures of human intercourse and the enjoyment of beautiful objects.' Moore believed this to be self-evidently true. To Moore's duo, the young Keynes added love of knowledge.

Good actions were those which brought about good states of mind. Moore said that it is only for the 'sake of these things [the pleasures of human intercourse and the enjoyment of beautiful objects] – in order that as much of them as possible may at some time exist – that anyone can be justified in performing any private or public duty; that they are the *raison d'etre* of virtue; that it is they... that form the rational end of human action and the sole criterion of progress.'

The young Keynes saw two problems with this. Moore, he said, had failed to establish a rational basis for altruistic behaviour: there is 'no necessary connection' between individual and universal goodness. 'For my goodness and the goodness of the Universe both seem to have a claim upon me and claims which I cannot easily reduce to common terms and weight against one another upon a common balance.' The rival claims on Keynes, we may say, were those of Bloomsbury and Whitehall.

Secondly, because 'we never have the opportunity of direct inspection [of other people's states of mind], it is impossible to tell what kinds of action increase the goodness of the Universe as a whole'. Moore's criterion of public action is inferior to Bentham's, because it is almost impossible, by reference to it, to establish whether ethical progress is taking place. Specifically, good states of mind do not depend, in any direct way, on good states of the world.

Moore provided a bridge to social reform with his doctrine of organic unity. The main purpose of this principle, as Keynes described it, was to limit the power to sum goodness by reference to isolated states of consciousness alone. In judging the goodness of a state of affairs, reference had to be made to time as well as to the objects of experience. Keynes decomposed Moore's 'complex wholes' into states of mind which were intrinsically good and objects which he called 'fit' or 'desirable'. Such objects need have no ethical value of their own. But, if they did not exist, the value of the experience would be less good than if they did. The social reformer could then claim that by improving the quality of the objects of experience he was increasing the ethical goodness of the universe. It follows straightforwardly from Moore that goodness is increased, *ceteris paribus*, by an increase in the amount of beauty. Keynes acted on this belief both as a philanthropist, builder of the Cambridge Arts theatre, and by accepting the job of first chairman of the Arts Council. In the depth of the depression, he also indicated that a programme of public investment, inspired by Moore's principles, would seek to endow Britain's cities 'with all the appurtenances of art and civilisation' and make them 'the greatest works of man in the world'. A follower of Moore might also interest himself in raising standards of education and of comfort in so far as these improved the intelligence, sensibility, and comeliness of the population.

The snag comes with Moore's class of 'mixed goods', in which good states of mind *depend* on the existence of bad states of affairs. Feelings of pity, courage, justice, which have positive ethical value, could be said to depend on the existence of suffering, danger, injustice. To the extent that social reform rids the world of bad states of affairs, it may be decreasing the total of ethical goodness. Social reformers may regard such considerations as trivial when weighed against avoidable suffering and oppression. The fact that Keynes was alert to them shows his intellectual honesty; it also helps explain his limited passion for social reform.

It was another problem arising from Moore's discussion of duty which led Keynes to spend, as he put it, 'all the leisure of many years' on the study of probability. We ought, Moore said, to behave in such a way as to bring about the greatest possible amount of goodness in the universe. But our knowledge of the effects of our actions is bound to be, at best, probabilistic. Since it was impossible to know the probable effects of actions stretching into a remote future, the best we could do in most cases, Moore argued, was to follow moral rules which were generally useful and generally practised, as Hume had suggested. This conclusion stuck in the young Keynes's gullet. 'Before heaven', he recalled in 1938, 'we claimed to be our own judge in our own case.' He set out to discover a rational basis for individual judgements of probability. In a paper he read to the Apostles on 23 January 1904, he said Moore was confusing knowledge of probabilities with knowledge of relative frequencies of occurrence. He was claiming that if we do not know for certain that any good we can achieve in the near future will not be outweighed by harm in the far future we have no rational basis for individual judgement. Keynes said this was wrong. All we have to have is *no reason to believe* that any immediate good we achieve would be overturned by distant consequences. Ignorance was not a barrier to individual judgement, but a way of neutralizing the unknown. By applying the 'principle of indifference' – assigning equiprobabilities to alternatives about which we have equal (including zero) evidence – we can extend the field of probability judgements. More generally, probabilistic knowledge was a kind of logical knowledge, concerning the 'bearing of evidence' on conclusions. It was to do with the rationality of beliefs, not the conjuncture of events. Keynes's *Treatise on Probability*, eventually published in 1921, was the working out of this audacious insight.

The question Keynes asked was: what are the principles of rational choice and action when the future is unknown or uncertain? His concern, that is, is with the rationality of means, not of ends, though the rightness of actions had to be judged by reference to both. Keynes claimed that the mind could often

41

'reduce' uncertainty to probability, 'intuiting' that some outcomes are more or less likely than others; in his words, 'perceiving' a probability relation between the evidence (the premiss) and the conclusion of an argument. This perception sanctions a 'degree of belief' in the conclusion. The logic he proposes is that of partial entailment.

Keynes's view of probability as logical *insight* was conceived as an attack on the dominant theory of his day – the frequency theory – which said that probability was a fact of nature: if one in ten smokers dies of cancer, the probability of smokers dying of cancer is 10%. The identification of frequency with probability, Keynes wrote, 'is a very grave departure from the established use of words'; moreover, it assumes the 'inductive hypothesis' which cannot itself be derived from frequencies.

The point, above all, which Keynes wanted to establish is that our knowledge of probabilities is more extensive than our knowledge of frequencies. By the same token, our knowledge of probabilities is only to a limited extend numerical knowledge – knowledge of ratios. Logical intuition, acting on evidence, can in most cases do no better than to discern that one conclusion is more likely than another, without being able to discern how much more or how much less likely. We have only a limited individual insight into the nature of the universe. Keynes allowed for unknown probabilities, arising from the impossibility in some cases of comparing probabilities based on different arguments. In deciding whether to take an umbrella on a walk, which should weigh more with us: the blackness of the clouds or the highness of the barometer? In such a case, 'it will be rational to allow caprice to determine us and to waste no time on the debate'. Again, ignorance should not been seen as a barrier to rational judgement.

Keynes's theory of probability is both optimistic about the power of human reason and pessimistic about the ability of reason to penetrate the secrets of the universe. He quoted Locke to the effect that 'in the greatest part of our concernment, God has afforded only the Twilight, as I may so say, of Probability, suitable, I presume, to the state of Mediocrity and Probationership He has been pleased to place us in here'.

In deciding what is rational to do, we need to take into account two further considerations independent of probability, which Keynes called 'the weight of argument' and 'moral risk'. By the first, Keynes meant roughly the *amount* of evidence supporting a probability judgement. This does not alter the probability, but can alter the amount of confidence we have in our judgement. Keynes's distinction between the rationality of a judgement and the confidence it is rational to have in it plays a key part in the discussion of investment psychology in *The General Theory*. The principle of moral risk suggests that it is more rational to aim for a smaller good which seems more probable of attainment than to aim for a larger one which seems less, when the two courses of action have equal probable goodness. Other things being equal, 'a high weight and the absence of risk increase *pro tanto* the desirability of the action to which they refer'. This argument provides the philosophical basis for Keynes's rejection of revolutionary change.

In preparing his dissertation on probability for publication, Keynes added extra sections on induction and statistical inference. A thoroughgoing empiricist, he wrote, cannot make use of induction without inconsistency, for the use of the inductive method requires that a prior probability be assigned to its validity. The 100-odd pages on statistical inference are remarkable chiefly for Keynes's attempt to reduce the domain of its validity to those sets of cases for which stable as opposed to average frequencies are available. This is the root of his objection to the misuse of econometrics. There is no doubt that Keynes's philosophic objection to induction gave a strong anti-empirical bias to his economics, despite his repeated calls for better data. While he aimed to choose models capable of explaining the 'facts of experience', his models are not derived from experience, but from introspection. In this respect, his method was much closer to that of the classical economists than to that of their 'institutionalist' critics.

Students of Keynes have only recently rescued his *Treatise on Probability* from its long neglect. This is part of the growing realization of the importance of Keynes's epistemology for understanding his theory of economic behaviour. One central debate concerns the status of his theory of probability. Was it, as Roderick O'Donnell claims, a Realist construction, or was it, as Anna Carabelli argues, a 'logic of opinion'? Keynes's insistence that probability was a 'real objective' relation, and that all rational beliefs have reference to true propositions, would seem to vindicate O'Donnell's approach, though Keynes later modified his opinion in response to criticisms by Frank Ramsey. A second issue concerns the epistemological continuity between the *Treatise on Probability* and *The General Theory*. Why, asks Athol Fitzgibbons, has the 'twilight of probability' turned by 1936 into the 'dark night' of uncertainty? The watershed of the First World War gives the answer. Finally, does Keynes, in *The General Theory*, see investment behaviour as rational or irrational? Here the main division is between those who see the 'conventional' investment strategy described by Keynes in *The General Theory* as a 'weak' form of rationality, and those who argue that Keynes believed investment behaviour to be irrational. This may be a non-debate, 'conventional' judgement of probabilities being what keeps investment reasonably steady, 'animal spirits' what produces the cycle.

These discussions are not just of historic interest. Keynes was the first economist to put uncertainty at the heart of the economic problem, and thus raise the issue of the scope and meaning of rationality in economics. Is rationality possible in an uncertain world, and how is it to be specified? The question for policy concerns the conditions which would need to be satisfied for the structure of the economy not to be viewed as radically uncertain by economic agents.

Keynes's theory of politics was set in the same conceptual framework as was his ethical and economic philosophy. The nearest he got to a systematic exposition was in a 100-page undergraduate essay on Edmund Burke, which he successfully submitted for the University Members' Prize for English Essay in 1904 – the same year as his earliest paper on probability. Keynes showed himself to be largely sympathetic to the views of the founder of British Conservatism. He approved of Burke's separation of ethics and politics, also his preference for present over future goods. He criticized him for excessive timidity as a reformer, and for undervaluing the claims of truth; in general for carrying reasonable propositions too far. The views he expressed in this undergraduate essay crop up time and again in his mature writings.

Burke's 'unparalleled political wisdom', according to Keynes, lay in the fact that he was the first thinker consistently to base a theory of politics on utilitiarianism rather than on abstract rights, though it was a utilitarianism 'modified' by the principle of equity – governments should avoid artificial discrimination against individuals or classes. He quotes him approvingly: 'The question with me is, not whether you have a right to render your people miserable, but whether it is not in your interest to make them happy.' Keynes adds: 'This is not a very recondite doctrine, but to Burke must be given the credit of first clearly and insistently enunciating it.' The most important consequence of this approach was Burke's championship of expediency as a central political principle – one which Keynes certainly approved. There is a jotting in Keynes's papers dating from the mid-1920s: 'It is fatal for a capitalist government to have principles. It must be opportunistic in the best sense of the word, living by accommodation and good sense. If a monarchical, plutocratic or other analogous form of government has principles, it will fall.' In policy-making, Keynes had a pronounced, but not extreme, preference for discretion over fixed rules, for reasons which can readily be inferred from his engagement with Burke.

Keynes accepted the view he attributed to Burke that the aim of politics was not to bring about states of affairs 'good intrinsically and in isolation', but to facilitate the pursuit of ethical goods by members of the community by guaranteeing conditions of 'physical calm, material comfort, and intellectual freedom'. Up to a point, the requirements of welfare and ethical goodness coincide. But Keynes never regarded politics as an arena for achieving ethical goals, and he placed limited ethical value on political passions.

Keynes endorses another key principle of Burke's: that the happiness or utility which governments should aim to maximize is short run not long run. This is a consequence of accepting the Moore–Burke criterion of 'moral risk' – 'Burke ever held, and held rightly, that it can seldom be right ... to sacrifice a present benefit for a doubtful advantage in the future.' The concept of moral risk was a guiding principle in Keynes's own statesmanship. It inoculated him equally against Communism and the sacrificial thinking implicit in much of orthodox economics.

However, Keynes thought Burke interpreted the 'moral risk' criterion too narrowly. In his essay of 1904, he criticized him for his 'preference for peace over truth, his extreme timidity in introducing present evil for the sake of future benefits, and his disbelief in men's acting rightly, except on the rarest occasions, because they have judged that it is right to act'. It was Burke's epistemological scepticism which forced him back on tradition. Burke denied the value of the pursuit of truth on the ground that it might disturb the peace of the Commonwealth (a present good) without giving any assurance of a greater benefit. This was a conclusion that Keynes wanted to resist. He argued, in the spirit of Mill, that 'whatever the immediate consequences of a new truth may be, there is a high probability that truth will in the long run

46

lead to better results than falsehood'. This was very much in line with his attack on Moore's argument for following generally accepted rules rather than using individual judgement. However, he conceded that the 'modern prejudice in favour of truth [may be] founded on somewhat insufficient bases'. Thus the *Treatise on Probability* may be regarded as his reply both to Moore and to Burke on this matter. Rationality was an important principle in Keynes's political philosophy. In the notion of policy informed by reason is a radical potential and optimistic outlook missing from classic Conservatism. It was his belief in the power of reason, and the possibility of rulers acting according to its dictates, which led him to allow considerable economic policy discretion to rulers.

Keynes's handling of Burke's views on property and democracy in the light of his 'maxims' of statesmanship is worth particular notice. Burke defended existing property rights on the double ground that redistribution of wealth would make no real difference to the poor, since they greatly outnumbered the rich, while at the same time it would 'considerably reduce in numbers those who could enjoy the undoubted benefits of wealth and who could confer on the state the advantages which the presence of wealthy citizens always brings'. Keynes felt this argument 'undoubtedly carries great weight ... and must always be one of the most powerful rejoinders to any scheme which has equalisation as its ultimate aim'. However, it was less valid if directed against 'any attempt to influence the channels in which wealth flows', and the relief of starvation or acute poverty. It was not valid, for example, against death duties 'whose object is to mulet great masses of accumulation', nor against the expropriation of feudal estates during the French Revolution. Burke was so often concerned to defend the 'outworks' of the property system, that he did not see that this might endanger the 'central' system itself.

This was a typical thought, typically expressed. In his *Tract on Monetary Reform* (1923), Keynes insisted that governments must have discretion to revise contracts between the living and the dead,

47

since 'the powers of uninterrupted usury are too great'. It was the 'absolutists of contract', he wrote, 'who are the parents of Revolution' – a good Burkean attitude, though one Burke sometimes ignored.

In the crises of the 1930s, Keynes came to think that more drastic interferences with the 'outworks' than he had contemplated in 1904 might be necessary to defend the 'central' system. Thus in *The General Theory* he proposed to bring about the 'euthanasia of the rentier' by making it impossible to take 'usury' on loans; he also defended the medieval usury laws which restricted interest to a maximum. Yet when his French correspondent Marcel Labordère pointed out to him that 'stable fortunes, the hereditary permanency of families and sets of families of various social standings are an invisible social asset on which every kind of culture is more or less dependent', Keynes readily replied: 'I fully agree with this, and I wish I had emphasised it in your words. The older I get the more convinced I am that what you say is true and important. But I must not allow you to make me too conservative.'

The issue of democracy, Keynes argued, involved two separate questions. Has the mass of people a right to direct self-government? Is it expedient and conducive to good government that there should be self-government? To both questions Burke had returned an 'uncompromising negative'. On the first, Keynes stood solidly with Burke. Government is simply a 'contrivance of human wisdom' to 'supply certain ... wants; and that is the end of the matter'. People are entitled to good government, not self-government – a doctrine which he would apply without question at the India Office. The more difficult question is whether self-government is necessary to good government, and here Keynes was more open than Burke. He agreed with him that 'the people' are incompetent to govern themselves and that Parliament must always be prepared to resist popular prejudice in the name of equity between individuals and classes. But he criticized Burke's 'dream of a representative class', and said that he underestimated the educative value of self-government. Nevertheless, Keynes doubted whether any 'rational or unprejudiced body of men' would have dared to make the experiment in universal suffrage had they not been 'under the influence of a fallacious notion concerning natural political rights'.

So far democracy had not disgraced itself. This was because its 'full force had not yet come into operation'. The existing system was oligarchic and plutocratic, rather than democratic. The assumption that it would continue in this way, with the addition of 'technical expertise' was the Achilles' heel of Keynes's political theory.

In his political philosophy, Keynes married two key elements of Burkean conservatism – contentment as the aim and risk avoidance as the method of government – to two key elements in reforming liberalism – a commitment to truth and belief in the possibility of rational individual judgement. He rejected both unthinking Conservatism and radical Socialism. This was very much the temper of the Middle Way which he espoused between the wars.

There has been much debate about what kind of Liberal Keynes was. Peter Clarke sees him as part of the pre-1914 'progressive' movement, uniting left-wing Liberals and moderate Socialists in a common redistributive, democratic programme. Against this, Michael Freeden argues that Keynes was a tough-minded, 'centrist' Liberal, grafting technocratic solutions onto an individualist stem. By confining state intervention to spaces left vacant by private enterprise, by 'jettisoning redistribution as a major field of socio-economic policy', and by 'de-democratizing' policy-making in favour of expert control, Keynes repudiated the distinctive features of 'progressive' Liberalism.

A case can be made out for both positions. What distances Keynes most obviously from the 'progressives' is his attitude to social justice. Keynes did not object (or object strongly) to the existing social order on the ground that it unfairly or unjustly distributed life-chances; rather that *laissez-faire* did not protect existing economic and social 'norms'. Injustice to him meant arbitrary changes in settled social arrangements, such as produced by changes in the value of money. He sympathized strongly with the miners at the time of the General Strike in 1926, because he saw them as victims of the return the previous year to the gold standard at an overvalued pound. Keynes transferred the problem of justice from the microeconomy to the macroeconomy. Injustice becomes a matter of uncertainty, justice a matter of contractual predictability. Redistribution plays a minor part in his social philosophy, and then only as part of the machinery of macroeconomic stabilization, not as a means to an ideal goal such as equality.

These attitudes emerge in his essay 'The End of *Laissez-Faire*', first delivered as a lecture at Oxford in 1924. The evils of the existing order arose largely from 'risk, uncertainty, and ignorance'. Their remedy required 'deliberate control of the currency and of credit by a central institution', the 'collection and dissemination of business facts', a 'coordinated act of intelligent judgment' concerning the aggregate volume of savings and their distribution between domestic and foreign investment, and a population policy 'which pays attention to innate quality as well as to . . . numbers'. What Keynes was after, as he later wrote in *The General Theory*, was to fill the gaps in the 'Manchester system'. As a criterion for public intervention Keynes offered the notion of a service or activity which was 'technically social' in the sense that only the State could provide it. Attached somewhat inconsistently to this set of arguments was an evolutionary perspective according to which the individualistic capitalism of family firms gave way to the 'socialized' capitalism of public utilities and large private corporations. Spontaneous industrial developments thus foreshadowed, and made possible, the conscious 'socialization of investment' Keynes was to advocate in *The General Theory*.

Despite the decline of the Liberals, Keynes refused to join either the Conservative or the Labour Parties. 'How could I bring myself to be a Conservative?' he asked himself in his essay of 1926, 'Am I a Liberal?'

> They offer me neither food nor drink – neither intellectual nor spiritual consolation ... [Conservatism] leads nowhere; it satisfies no ideal; it conforms to no intellectual standard; it is not even safe, or calculated to preserve from spoilers that degree of civilisation which we have already attained.

For a Liberal of Keynes's generation, the Conservative Party was the historic enemy, and remained so throughout the interwar years, despite the 'decency' of Stanley Baldwin. It was the party of stupidity, superstitition, and prejudice; the party of protectionism and jingoism. The Conservatives were also guardians of the reactionary moral code against which Keynes's generation had rebelled. As part of the agenda of Liberalism, Keynes listed 'Birth control and the use of contraceptives, marriage laws, the treatment of sexual offences and abnormalities, the economic position of women, the economic position of the family ... drug questions'. On all these matters of special concern to Bloomsbury and Hampstead, Conservatives – at least in public – upheld positions which he habitually dubbed 'medieval'.

He attributed the stupidity of Conservatism to its attachment to the hereditary principle. This also explained the inefficiency of many British firms. British capitalism was dominated by third-generation men. His initial respect for the Conservative leader, Stanley Baldwin, rapidly waned: 'There was an attraction at first that Mr. Baldwin should not be clever. But when he forever sentimentalizes about his own stupidity, the charm is broken,' he scribbled in 1925. Yet as late as 1936, he cited Baldwin 'as a model statesman who could bring about a modified socialism if his party would let him'.

If the Conservatives were the stupid party, Labour was the silly party. But at least much of its heart was in the right place. What was needed, Keynes often suggested, was Labour's head of steam yoked to the programme of reforming Liberalism. In much of his political writing, Keynes was engaged in a dialogue with the Labour movement. This sometimes involved him in a very ambiguous use of language, as he tried to distinguish his position from that of socialism and also to stress the compatibility between a range of Liberal and socialist aspirations. This ambiguity, which he seemed to see as a necessary part of his efforts at persuasion, makes it very hard to decide the question of how far Keynes would have been willing to go down the socialist road. In his lifetime, he never had to make the choice which confronted many people in the 1970s.

Keynes emphatically rejected socialism as an *economic* remedy for the ills of capitalism. Both classical economists and socialists, he often said, believed in the same 'laws of economics'. But whereas the former regarded them as true and inevitable, the latter saw them as true and intolerable. Keynes proposed to show they were not true. He added that the very fact that capitalism was 'socializing' itself made public ownership unnecessary.

Keynes objected to socialism's revolutionary strain. He understood that the bulk of the Labour Party were not 'Jacobins, Communists, Bolshevists', but he thought the malignity and envy of these groups affected the whole party, consorting ill 'with ideals to build up a true social republic'. In a debate with the Scottish Socialist Thomas Johnston in 1929, he argued that Labour had to 'put on an appearance of being against anyone who is more successful, more skilful, more industrious, more thrifty than the average ... This is most unjust and most unwise. It disturbs what is and always must be the strongest section of the community and throws them into the reactionary camp.'

Keynes explicitly rejected the class basis of socialist politics. A much quoted remark of his is: '[The Labour Party] is a class party, and the class is not my class. If I am going to pursue sectional interests at all, I shall pursue my own ... I can be influenced by what seems to be justice and good sense; but the *class* war will find me on the side of the *educated* bourgeoisie.' He was a leveller who wanted to level upwards not downwards. 'I want to give encouragement to all exceptional effort, ability, courage, character. I do not want to antagonize the successful, the exceptional'.

Finally, Keynes rejected Labour's anti-élitism. He felt that the intellectual elements in the Labour party will '[n]ever exercise adequate control; too much will always be decided by those who do not know *at all* what they are talking about'. The Conservatives were much better off in this respect, since 'the inner ring of the party can almost dictate the details and the technique of policy'. As his earliest writings show, Keynes believed in rule by a Platonic guardian class, constrained, but not dominated, by democracy.

Keynes admired three things about socialism: its passion for justice, the Fabian ideal of public service; and its utopianism, based on the elimination of the profit motive. Keynes had his own Utopia which inspired his work as an economist, expressed notably in his essay, 'Economic Possibilities for our Grandchildren', published in 1930. Here he outlines his vision of a society which is a paradise of abundance, leisure, beauty, grace, and variety, and in which 'love of money' comes to be regarded as a mental disease. But this Utopia owed more to Cambridge than to socialist philosophy (there is no obvious place in it for equality, fraternity, or democracy). Besides, it was to come about only after the economic problem was solved. Meanwhile, as Keynes put it, 'we must go on pretending that fair is foul and foul is fair; for foul is useful and fair is not'. In short, Keynes rejected socialism as a means; and as an end endorsed it only in his own idiosyncratic sense.

That occasionally penetrating observer of interwar British culture, Dmitri Mirsky, gave a Marxist interpretation of Keynes's philosophy of practice in his book *The Intelligentsia of Great Britain*. The intellectual aristocracy, he said, not being directly involved in the production process, could consider itself outside or above class. In economics, it demanded organization, which it called socialism, but in individual life it wanted more freedom, which chained it to capitalism.

Today such antitheses seem less compelling. Few people now believe that socialism, in the sense which Keynes rejected it, is relevant to our economic problems. The question is whether Keynes's Middle Way is still relevant. He believed that there would be a growing deficiency of aggregate demand in mature capitalist economies, as investment opportunities flag, but savings habits appropriate to the individualistic era persist. Public intervention would be needed to maintain investment demand, redistribute income to high consuming groups, and rearrange conditions of work and pay in order gradually to increase the attactions of leisure as science increased the power to produce. Otherwise, he warned, the Great Depression of 1929–32 would be the foretaste of permanent semi-slump. His political ideas were embedded in his economic response to British mass unemployment in the 1920s, which we must now examine.

Chapter 3
The monetary reformer

Keynes's discussion of the British unemployment problem in the 1920s took place within the framework of the quantity theory of money. He had no doubt that fluctuations in business activity could be prevented by appropriate monetary policy. The quantity theorists of Keynes's day were monetary reformers who wanted to use the theory of money to stabilize economic activity. The quantity theory of money was the first theory of short-run macroeconomic stabilization.

On the face of it, this is curious, because the quantity theory of money is a theory relating the supply of money to the *price level* at which goods are bought, not to the *quantity* of goods produced. Yet, as a matter of observed fact, changes in money and prices *were* associated with fluctuations in quantity of output and employment, and this needed to be explained. For the first thirty years or so of this century, economists, including Keynes, tried to use what they called the quantity theory of money to explain fluctuations in output. They did so, partly because of the observed correlation between monetary events and fluctuations in business activity, and partly because monetary policy offered the most promising parameter of action for those who wanted to manage, but not destroy, the capitalist system. In the 1930s, Keynes abandoned the quantity theory approach to the explanation of short-run fluctuations in output. In *The General Theory*, money still retains its power to disturb the real economy. But its disturbing power arises from its function as a store of value rather than as a means of exchange. This had the further consequence of calling into question the reliability of monetary policy as an instrument of economic management.

The quantity theory was based on the transactions view of money. Money was a medium of exchange, a means of effecting purchases and sales of goods and services. It has no other purpose, at least in a 'modern' economy with a stable legal and political order and a developed banking system. This being so, a change in the quantity (or value) of money could disturb a previous equilibrium only if it produced non-proportionate changes in agents' money stocks. This indeed was the assumption of those who used the quantity theory to analyse economic fluctuations. Rising prices, it was typically said, benefit investors and entrepreneurs at the expense of savers and wage-earners; falling prices, the reverse. This argument hinged on the distinction between flexible and non-flexible prices. Thus wage rates were assumed to be 'fixed' or at least 'sticky' in the short run, selling prices 'flexible'. At the same time, the transactions view of money made stabilizing the price level seem deceptively easy. Money had no utility other than as a means of effecting transactions. People 'demanded' it, Keynes used to say before 1914, only to get rid of it as quickly as possible. All the central authority had to do was to ensure an appropriate supply of money and all would be well. From before the First World War up to and including his *Treatise on Money*, Keynes's work was in this tradition, though by the end it was becoming increasingly problematic for him.

Two forms of the quantity theory were available when Keynes started work as an economist – Irving Fisher's 'transactions' version, and the Cambridge 'cash balances' approach, developed by Alfred Marshall, who taught Keynes his economics. Keynes used both in his pre-1914 lectures, saying they come to 'practically the same thing'. Fisher's equation of exchange, $MV = PT$, states that, in any period, the quantity of money (M) times its velocity of circulation – the average number of times per period which a pound or dollar is spent (V) – equals the average price of each transaction (P) multiplied by the total number of transactions (T). All this means is that the value of what is spent is equal to the value of what is bought, hardly a surprising conclusion. Three further propositions are needed to convert the equation of exchange into a theory of the price level. First, causation runs from money to prices. Secondly, the velocity of circulation is determined independently of the money supply by the community's level of income and payments habits. These change only slowly. Thirdly, the volume of transactions is determined independently of the quantity of money by 'real' forces. If these propositions are true, any change in the quantity of money will lead to a proportional change in the price level.

In the Marshallian 'cash balances' version of the quantity theory, $M = k$ PT, M, P, and T have the same meaning as before, and k – the fraction of the community's wealth or income (Marshall tended to use the terms interchangeably) which on average is held as cash during the period – is the reciprocal of V, the velocity of circulation. The Cambridge equation emphasized not the spending of money, but the role of money as a temporary abode of purchasing power between selling and buying. It was a bridge to the 'store of value' function of money by pointing to individual motives for holding liquid assets and suggesting that they could be further analysed.

It did not point too far in this direction to the pre-war Keynes. He regarded the quantity theory of money not just as a logical exercise – as a statement of the conditions necessary for it to be true – but as a realistic set of assumptions about the real world. He certainly believed that the causation ran from money to prices, castigating 'businessmen' and 'popular opinion' for holding the contrary view. He believed that the 'rapidity of circulation' or 'demand for money balances to hold' is institutionally determined and not subject to erratic shifts. He also accepted the third proposition – that the volume of transactions is determined by 'real' forces. All this being so, he accepted the quantity theory in both its versions. At the same time he recognized that fluctuations in prices can have temporary effects on the velocity of circulation and the state of trade, though his discussion was distinctly perfunctory.

Keynes's account of the 'transmission mechanism' from money to prices is strictly Marshallian, indeed he accused Fisher of failing to specify a mechanism. An increase in the central bank's gold reserves leads to lower interest rates. Entrepreneurs increase their borrowing; it is the spending of their new deposits which first causes prices to rise, and this stimulus 'gradually spreads to all parts of the community, until the new gold is needed to finance a volume of real trade no larger ... than before'. The price level is what equilibrates the 'demand for cash' with the 'supply of cash'. The important point, though, is that it takes *time* for an injection of money to have its final effect on prices, and it is while prices are adjusting to changes in the money supply that trade may be boosted or depressed. It follows also that under the gold standard 'the supply of purchasing power depends upon banking and gold jointly'.

The pre-1914 monetary reformers aimed to reduce the influence of gold on the 'supply of purchasing power'. Stabilization of the price level required the quantity of money to be under the control of the central monetary authority. But where legal tender money consisted of gold coins, the long-run value of money was determined by unregulated conditions of supply and demand in the gold market. The late 19th-century fall in the price level was widely attributed to the increased cost of extracting gold from the depleted Californian and Australian mines, as well as to increased gold hoarding in India. Technically, the quantity of gold money was not an exogenous variable. Reformers devised schemes to vary the quantity of gold in money – the tabular standard of Marshall, the compensated dollar of Fisher were examples – so as to achieve a more stable price level. The Swedish economist Knut Wicksell took

the bull by the horns: the ideal international standard would be a
paper standard, giving central banks complete control over the
money supply. In his *Interest and Prices*, published in German in
1898, Wicksell argued that 'there is a certain rate of interest on
loans which is neutral in respect to commodity prices, and tends
neither to raise them nor lower them'. He called this the 'natural'
(or profit) rate. The crux of Wicksell's argument against the gold
standard was that it prevented the central bank from adjusting the
market rate of interest to changes in the 'natural' rate. Keynes did
not pick up this thread till 1930. But even before 1914 he echoed
Irving Fisher in advocating a 'more rational and stable' standard
than the gold standard. In his *Indian Currency and Finance*
(1913), he proposed a reform of the Indian banking system to
increase the seasonal elasticity of the stock of rupees, and looked
forward to the day when gold-based currencies would be restricted
to one or two countries, whose central banks would 'manage' what
was, in effect, a fiduciary international standard. 'It is not likely', he
wrote, 'that we shall leave permanently the most intimate
adjustments of our economic organism at the mercy of a lucky
prospector, a new chemical process, or a change of ideas in Asia,'
and 'A preference for a tangible reserve currency is . . . a relic of a
time when governments were less trustworthy in these matters
than they now are.' His successive plans for managed currencies up
to Bretton Woods none the less retained a 'constitutional monarch'
role for gold as the foundation of a pegged exchange-rate system
and ultimate safeguard against inflation.

Though 'constitutional' schemes for reforming the gold standard
failed before the First World War, it was becoming an increasingly
'managed' standard as central banks used a variety of devices to
offset or neutralize gold flows in the interests of domestic price
stability. The effect of an inflow or outflow of gold was seen to
depend within wide limits on the action of the central bank. This
led pre-war monetary theory to give increasing emphasis to the
role of banking policy in determining the money supply. Attention
switched from the influence of gold movements on prices to that of

credit flows. The quantity theory of money was becoming a quantity theory of credit. In a paper 'How Far are Bankers Responsible for the Alternations of Crisis and Depression?', read to the Political Economy Club in December 1913, Keynes argued that banks can lend to entrepreneurs without borrowing the equivalent amount from savers; credit creation can be an independent source of inflation. However, when investment 'runs ahead' of saving, there has to be a depression to enable saving to 'catch up'. These ideas were to be taken up again in the mid-1920s. However, as long as it could be assumed that the central bank had the means to regulate the rate of credit creation by the commercial banks, the existence of credit money posed no danger to its ability to 'control the money supply'.

Much of the theory and practice of monetary reform was in place before 1914; but Keynes's war experience and its monetary consequences enriched his theory and gave his policy discussion an urgency it never had before the war. He had advised the Treasury during the banking crisis of July–August 1914, explaining the crisis in terms of an 'unusual demand for money' by the banking system, following the failure of foreign remittances and the stock-market collapse. The crisis was averted by the Bank of England purchasing bills from the market. The duty of the central bank to act as 'lender of the last resort' to the banking system had been part of central banking theory since the time of Walter Bagehot, who enunciated the doctrine in his classic, *Lombard Street* (1870), and Keynes accepted it without question. His wartime Treasury experience also led him to identify inflation as the mechanism by which a needy government, too weak to tax honestly, can transfer real resources to itself. In a wartime correspondence with the economist Edwin Cannan of the London School of Economics, Keynes denied that inflation could be overcome simply by limiting the note issue. He wrote to Cannan on 28 January 1918:

> The excessive issue of currency notes and the degree of inflation which exists, connected partly with this note issue, and partly

with the increase in bank credits, seems to me due to national
expenditure being on a scale beyond what the government can pay
for by taxes and loans ... As long as this is the case, regulation of the
note issue is impossible. ... It is more scientific I think to attribute
the inflation to the excess expenditure by Government and to hold
that it can only be cured by the diminution of expenditure public and
private.

More generally, the topics which gained in prominence as
compared to pre-war were those arising from wartime inflation,
post-war currency disorders, and the overhang of wartime debt.
The war and post-war inflations were explained along quantity
theory lines by inflationary government finance. The 'purchasing
power parity' theory of the exchanges was developed by the
Swedish economist Gustav Cassel to explain the link between
domestic price inflation and exchange depreciation. The issue of
Germany's capacity to pay reparations generated a technical
discussion on the nature of the 'transfer problem'. Keynes took an
active part in all these discussions. Of particular note is his warning
against inflation. In his *Economic Consequences of the Peace*, he
quoted with approval a remark attributed to Lenin that 'there is no
subtler, no surer means of overturning the existing basis of society
than to debauch the currency'. The immense volatility of prices and
exchange rates in the immediate post-war period, as well as the
change in the balance of power between the United States and
Europe, formed the historical raw material of his *Tract on
Monetary Reform* (1923).

The explicit goal of *A Tract on Monetary Reform* was domestic
price stability. Only stable prices could produce stable or normal
business activity. 'I regard the stability of prices, credit and
employment as of paramount importance,' Keynes wrote.
His argument was that fluctuations in the value of money trigger
short-run fluctuations in business activity, because they change
class income shares and disturb settled expectations. Falling prices
are said to injure employment, both because money-wages are

fixed in the short run, and because falling prices depress expectations of sales proceeds. 'It is worse, in an impoverished world', Keynes wrote, 'to provoke unemployment than to disappoint the *rentier*.' This combination of institutional and theoretical arguments was typical of Keynes. It is one of the sources of the many disputes about what he 'really' meant. The important point being made was that price stability was necessary for contractual predictability, which was related to economic stability. Monetary reform was an antidote to social revolution.

Four particular points of interest stand out from the *Tract*. First, Keynes attacked the policy of restoring the gold standard. In this, he took to its logical conclusion the argument of the monetary reformers that stable domestic prices might be inconsistent with stable exchange rates. Instead of domestic prices being required to adjust to the exchange rate, the exchange rate should be adjusted to a domestic price level consistent with a 'normal' (that is, reasonably full) level of employment. A scintillating section on the forward market in exchanges is designed to show that traders can 'hedge' much more easily against exchange-rate fluctuations than can producers against domestic price fluctuations. Thus 'contracts and business expectations, which presume a stable exchange, may be far fewer, even in a trading country such as England, than those which presume a stable level of internal prices'.

The crucial context of the argument was the new dominance of the United States. 'With the existing distribution of the world's gold, the reinstatement of the gold standard means, inevitably, that we surrender the regulation of our price level and the handling of the credit cycle to the Federal Reserve Board of the United States.' The American monetary authorities would determine their monetary policy by reference to domestic conditions, not to the requirements of other countries like Britain. The best solution was to divide the world into 'managed' sterling and dollar currency blocs. 'So long as the Federal Reserve Board was successful in keeping dollar prices steady the objective of keeping sterling prices steady would be identical with the objective of keeping the dollar-sterling exchange steady.' Gold would be retained as the ultimate means of settling international debts.

Secondly, Keynes thought that stable prices could be achieved by monetary policy alone. He did not see wage pressure as a complicating factor. Nor did he query the interest-elasticity of investment, though he did understand that there were expectational limits to real interest-rate changes – an insight he did not exploit till *The General Theory*. Controlling inflation was mainly a matter of stopping inflationary government finance.

Thirdly, Keynes was a broad, not narrow, money man. The right policy was 'to watch and to control the creation of credit and to let the creation of currency follow suit'. This was because the quantity of cash was a backward-looking indicator. It was not the past rise in prices but the future rise which had to be counteracted. The wartime debate between Keynes and Edwin Cannan foreshadows the debates between the 'broad' and 'narrow' money versions of monetarism in the 1980s. The problem of which kind of money to track or monitor was posed for the first time.

Finally, Keynes favoured discretionary management, rejecting a money-supply rule as unsuitable for controlling the credit cycle. He wrote down a simplified form of Pigou's monetary equation, $n = p$ $(k + rk')$, where n is currency notes and other forms of cash in circulation, p is the index number of the cost of living, k is the real value of cash in hand, k' the real value of bank deposits including overdrafts, and r the ratio of the banking system's reserves to liabilities. The quantity theory, he said, was based on the assumption that 'a *mere* change in the quantity of the currency cannot affect k, r, and k'' – that is to say, that these variables are determined independently of n. Consequently a change in n will cause an equiproportionate movement in p. Double the quantity of money, and you double the price level.

> Now, 'in the long run' this is probably true.... But this *long run* is
> a misleading guide to current affairs. *In the long run* we are all
> dead. Economists set themselves too easy, too useless a task if in
> tempestuous seasons they can only tell us that when the storm
> is long past the ocean is flat again.

When prices are rising, people reduce their 'real balances' (k
and k'); when prices are falling they increase them. Central banks
vary their reserve requirements to offset gold flows.

Given the short-run instability of what would now be called the
'demand for money' function, there was no stable short-run
relationship between the money stock and money national income.
Keynes saw that 'the mood of the public and the business world'
could exert an independent influence on the price level. In trying to
stabilize prices, the monetary authority had to be prepared to act
on both the supply of money *and* the demand for money; in
Keynes's language, its duty consisted in 'exercising a stabilising
influence over k and k', and, in so far as this fails or is
impracticable, in deliberately varying n and r so as to
counterbalance the movement of k and k''. The algebraic
symbolism made the task of monetary management seem all too
easy. Any tendency for real balances to increase can be
counteracted by lowering bank rate 'because easy lending
diminishes the advantages of keeping a margin for contingencies
in cash'. The central bank can vary the amount of cash it makes
available to the banking system by buying and selling securities.
As long 'as we refrain from inflationary finance on the one hand
and a return to an unregulated gold standard on the other',
the control of the money supply and thus of the price level will be
in the hands of the central bank.

The *Tract on Monetary Reform* recognizes that monetary shocks
can affect business activity because of uncertainty about the future
course of prices. Quantity theorists had tended to argue that it was
only *unanticipated* changes in the price level which produced

disturbances to proportionality. Keynes argued, more realistically, that even if price rises or falls are *expected*, uncertainty about the extent of the movement can affect business behaviour. Keynes has identified the central importance of uncertainty: but to what price, or particular set of prices, to attach it in order to explain the rhythms of trade was a problem which was to occupy him over his next two books.

These deeper questions were hardly tested by Winston Churchill's decision to return sterling to the gold standard in April 1925. In his pamphlet *The Economic Consequences of Mr. Churchill*, published in July, Keynes treated the decision straightforwardly as a monetary shock inflicted by the government on the industry of the country. His argument was that returning the pound to its pre-war parity with the dollar – £1 = $4.86 – overvalued sterling by 10%, requiring a 10% fall in the money costs of production if the existing volume of British exports was to be maintained. This would meet with intense worker resistance, which could only be overcome, Keynes argued, by 'intensifying unemployment' without limit. Keynes said that these economics of the 'juggernaut' could be short-circuited by means of a 'national treaty' to reduce wages and other incomes by agreement. He suspected, though, that government policy would actually produce a 'jammed' low-employment economy. The government would carry deflation far enough to provoke, but not cure, unemployment, and borrow from abroad to plug the export shortfall.

This is roughly what happened. By 1928, Keynes was producing what was to be his standard summary of the whole episode:

> we have deflated prices by raising the exchange value of sterling and by controlling the volume of credit; *but we have not deflated costs* . . . The fundamental blunder of the Treasury and Bank of England has been due, from the beginning, to their belief that if they looked after the deflation of prices the deflation of costs would look after itself.

Less than a year after the *Tract* was published, Keynes started a new book which he first called 'The Theory of Money and Credit'. It was to be a study of the theory of money in relation to the 'credit cycle'. In the *Tract*, Keynes had given the monetary authority the duty of offsetting fluctuations in 'cash balances'. But the composition of these balances, and causes of their fluctuations, had not been analysed. In tackling the problem, Keynes reverted to the ideas of his paper of 1913. Banks can lend more or less than the public want to save. The task of monetary policy is to keep bank-lending equal to saving intentions.

In analysing the relationship between 'bank money' and saving, Keynes was greatly influenced by his Cambridge colleague Dennis Robertson, who was then writing his *Banking Policy and the Price Level*, published in 1926. His intellectual engagement with Robertson at this point was decisive for the development of his own ideas. Robertson was, above all, a business-cycle theorist, drawing on a rich Continental literature to explain why the growth of wealth was spasmodic. Keynes was permanently influenced by two features of business-cycle theory: first, the view that the business cycle is an investment cycle, caused by fluctuations in the expected profitability of capital goods; secondly, that this 'real' cycle is amplified to boom and slump by monetary factors – particularly by the failure of monetary policy to keep investment equal to saving. Robertson thought that 'real' business fluctuations were inseparable from progress. He wanted to use monetary policy, though, to eliminate 'inappropriate' fluctuations in real activity. This might entail abandoning the goal of price stability.

Keynes and Robertson started out by agreeing that only credit inflation or deflation could make investment diverge from voluntary saving. Much of Robertson's *Banking Policy and the Price Level*, including its array of peculiar terms, was devoted to showing how different forms of non-voluntary spending and saving could be brought about by credit operations. This included the idea that temporary inflation creates an investment fund by 'forcing' people to consume less and therefore 'save' more. The famous doctrine of 'forced saving', first stated by Thomas Joplin after the Napoleonic wars, was rediscovered from observation of how the government 'confiscated' its citizens' incomes without taxing them in the First World War. Basically, the government pre-empts a slice of national output by spending an additional amount of new money created at its behest through the banking system. The additional spending raises the general level of prices (having generated excess demand at the previous level of prices) and private economic actors find themselves needing (or wishing) to *hold* rather than to respend the additional money created, because the increase in the price level has raised their requirements for nominal cash holdings relative to the physical volume of transactions. Attempts by the government to repeat the process will eventually bring an accelerating inflationary spiral, as private actors anticipate and try to thwart the government's purposes by adjusting their own spending.

Keynes's new book started along this track, but eventually left it. He explained to Robertson in 1931:

> When you were writing your *Banking Policy and the Price Level*, and we were discussing it, we both believed that inequalities between saving and investment – using those terms with the degree of vagueness with which we used them at that date – only arose as a result of what one might call an act of inflation or deflation on the part of the banking system. I worked on this basis for quite a time, but in the end I came to the conclusion that this would not do. As a result of getting what were, in my opinion, more clear definitions of saving and investment, I found that the salient phenomena could come about without any overt act on the part of the banking system.

Robertson had talked about savings being either invested or hoarded. Keynes emphasized a third alternative: savings neither invested nor hoarded but used to buy existing assets. Thus saving can 'run ahead' of investment (defined as buying *new* capital equipment), without any slowdown in the overall velocity of circulation. This line of thought was influenced by the speculative Wall Street bull market of 1927–9. Keynes lost faith in the ability of the 'transactions' version of the quantity theory of money to explain short-term business fluctuations. What was important for employment was not the total of transactions in a period, but whether or not money income was being spent on current output.

Another crucial distinction in the *Treatise*, between 'foreign investment' and 'foreign lending', was influenced by Keynes's involvement in the debate on German reparation payments. The fact that British savings, uninvested at home, were being lent abroad, did not mean that all savings were being invested, because, with a fixed exchange rate, any attempt to lend more abroad than Britain's export surplus allowed would cause a drain of gold and force a rise in bank rate at home. This would cause domestic investment to fall by the amount of the excess of foreign lending over the current account surplus.

What Keynes and Robertson were both trying to do, not yet very successfully, was to integrate saving-investment analysis with the theory of money, rather than maintain the rigid separation between them which was a feature of the classical or quantity theory approach.

In his *The Keynesian Revolution in the Making* (1988), Peter Clarke has persuasively argued that the publication of the *Treatise* was held up, and its analysis altered, by Keynes's need to confront the 'Treasury View' developed in 1928–9 to refute Lloyd George's plan to cure unemployment by a programme of loan-financed public works. The author of this notorious 'View' was Ralph Hawtrey. In an article in *Economica* in March 1925, Hawtrey had argued that, with a fixed money supply, any loan raised by the government for public works would 'crowd out' (in today's parlance) an equivalent amount of private spending. Employment could be increased only by credit expansion – borrowing from the banks. But it was the credit expansion which was important, not the public works, which Hawtrey condemned as a 'piece of ritual'. From late 1928, the Treasury, primed by Hawtrey, started to argue that 'What Keynes is after, of course, is a definite inflation of credit' – which was inconsistent with the maintenance of the gold standard. The prime minister, Stanley Baldwin, was fed the lines: 'we must *either* take existing money *or* create new money'. Since the latter was ruled out by the gold standard, the crowding-out argument seemed to hold. Keynes as yet had not developed his consumption function/multiplier analysis to refute it; and even if he had developed it, its applicability in the absence of cheap money would have been open to question.

He took a stride towards developing it in *Can Lloyd George Do It*; a pamphlet he wrote with Hubert Henderson in May 1929. To the Treasury argument that no savings were available to finance *additional* investment Keynes replied that this assumed full employment of all resources. The unemployed resources included savings which had not 'materialized' owing to the 'want of prosperity'. This was an odd way of putting it. But the thought Keynes was expressing – in the language of the *Treatise* – was that business losses caused by recession made the national savings less than they would have been had entrepreneurs been earning 'normal' profits. The implication of this was that any policy (including a loan-financed public works' programme) which succeeded in restoring a 'normal' level of income would create the saving needed to finance the investment.

Corresponding to this, the employment-creating effects of additional government spending would not be limited to those directly employed on government projects. For every man put to work building a road or a house, at least another would find a job supplying the inputs required. Furthermore, the additional purchasing power thus created would exert a 'cumulative force' on trade activity, making the employment effects of a given capital expenditure far larger than the direct and indirect effects indicated above, though 'it is not possible to measure effects of this character with any sort of precision'. The 'employment multiplier', worked out by Richard Kahn in 1931, was an attempt to measure these 'cumulative' effects.

The more direct approach to the analysis of output and employment opened up by Keynes's confrontation with the Treasury View in 1929 had, in a sense, made much of the *Treatise on Money* redundant, from his point of view, when it was finally published in October 1930. Nevertheless it is a book with a wealth of institutional understanding of financial and money markets, some fundamental theory, and some theoretical loose ends on which Keynes soon started to work.

It is a difficult book to summarize. Its central theoretical proposition is that saving and investment are done by two different sets of people for different motives and there is no automatic mechanism in a credit money economy to keep them equal. There is a rate of profit on capital (which Keynes, following Wicksell, called the 'natural' rate) and there is a rate of interest on loans – the 'market' rate. But the market rate demanded by lenders may be higher or lower than the profit rate available to or expected by investors. Thus the possibility arises that not all income earned will get spent by consumers or investors.

The practical import of all this is that the only balancer a credit-money economy has is banking *policy*. Under the gold standard the Bank of England was prevented from setting bank rate low enough to allow a level of investment equal to what the community wanted to save: hence mass unemployment. Crucial to this demonstration is Keynes's switch in emphasis from the stock of money to the flow of spending. It was insufficiency of spending on investment relative to the rate of saving which caused both the price level to fall *and* people to be unemployed.

Fundamental in terms of economic psychology is Keynes's break from the classical view of saving as providing an automatic route to investment. He dismissed the 'abstinence' theory of economic progress in a couple of superb paragraphs:

> It has been usual to think of the accumulated wealth of the world as having been painfully built up out of the voluntary abstinence of individuals from the immediate enjoyment of consumption which we call thrift. But it should be obvious that mere abstinence is not enough by itself to build cities or drain fens . . . It is enterprise which builds and improves the world's possessions . . . If enterprise is afoot, wealth accumulates whatever may be happening to thrift; and if enterprise is asleep, wealth decays whatever thrift may be doing.

> Thus, thrift may be the handmaid and nurse of enterprise. But equally she may not be. And, perhaps, even usually she is not. For enterprise is connected with thrift not directly, but at one remove; and the link which should join them is frequently missing. For the engine which drives enterprise is not thrift, but profit.

Unfortunately, Keynes tried to formalize these pathbreaking ideas in 'Fundamental Equations', whose origins lie in an earlier phase of the book, when he was still trying to use the quantity theory of money to explain business fluctuations. Throughout the *Treatise* the reader is being tripped up by dead skins which Keynes had sloughed off while writing it. To adapt the new ideas to the older ones critical terms like 'income', 'profits', and 'saving' are used in special ways. Though Keynes is trying to explain how, if interest rates are prevented from falling, a slump can develop and persist, the spotlight is on changing price levels, not on changes in output and employment.

The three sets of relevant definitions are: (*a*) the community's money income (otherwise the 'normal' or equilibrium earnings of the factors of production, or costs of production); (*b*) profits, which are defined as the difference between costs of production and

71

selling prices, and exclude entrepreneurs' 'normal' earnings; and (c) saving, defined as that part of the community's 'normal' income withheld from consumption. The purpose of excluding profits and losses (which Keynes also calls 'windfalls') from income is to segregate the variable causing output to expand or contract. But the attempt results in non-operational definitions of income and saving which were the cause of much misunderstanding. We have the illusion that they stay constant even though profits are positive or negative. The idea that aggregate saving can 'run ahead' or 'fall behind' investment depended entirely on the way income and saving are defined.

Formally, the *Treatise* is an attempt to capture, in a set of equations, the dynamics of an economy in transition from one (consumer) price level to another. We are presented, on the one side, with the flow of money earned by the factors of production in producing consumption and investment goods, and, on the other, its division into the parts which are spent on buying consumption goods and those which are saved. The price level of consumption goods is stable if the proportions of money earned in producing consumption and investment goods are the same as the division of spending between current consumption and saving.

In this situation, costs of production equal the selling prices of consumption goods; profits are zero; saving equals the cost of investment: all true by definition. If, on the other hand, people spend less on buying consumption goods than they have earned producing them, consumer prices fall. In this situation, by definition, costs exceed prices; profits are negative by the same amount; and saving 'runs ahead' of the cost of investment.

This tortured approach was designed to emphasize one key point. If what people want to save exceeds the cost of investment the economy as a whole becomes depressed unless something is happening simultaneously to raise the *value* or profitability of investment. The required transfer of spending from consumption to investment does not happen automatically. Whether it happens depends on 'a different set of considerations': whether the anticipated profitability of investment is going up, or the rate of interest falling, or a mixture of both, at the same time.

Depression arises if the incentive to buy *new* pieces of capital equipment is insufficient to absorb the rate of saving out of 'normal' income – in other words if the expected rate of profit falls below the market rate set by the banking system. Keynes applies the uncertainty analysis started in the *Tract* to a specific set of prices – those of capital goods. It is the oscillations of the 'natural' rate of interest, driven by volatile expectations, around the market rate set by banking practices which explains the business cycle.

The *Treatise* contains the first of Keynes's two famous discussions of the psychology of the stock exchange, much influenced by the collapse of the long 'bull' market on Wall Street in 1929. The key idea is that part of savings is 'held' for speculative purposes, because of uncertainty about the future value of capital assets. If the price of shares on the stock-market is expected to go up, savings will be redistributed from 'hoards' to 'securities', and vice versa if the price of shares is expected to fall. When most investors are 'bulls' you get a stock-market boom; when most of them are 'bears' you have a stock-market slump. Thus a 'speculative' motive for money balances to hold is identified in the *Treatise*, but it does not become Keynes's liquidity-preference theory till *The General Theory*.

Keynes does not doubt that the 'gap' between investment and 'saving' can be cured by lowering the market rate of interest. But this was prevented by the gold standard. In an open economy under a fixed exchange-rate system, the rate of interest has two jobs to do which may be incompatible: to regulate investment and to manage the balance of payments. If a community's desire to lend savings abroad exceeded its net export surplus, gold would be exported, which the monetary authority would have to offset by raising the rate of interest, thus increasing the cost of capital at home. The ultimate effect of a high bank rate would be a decline in 'efficiency wages' (national income), making possible an enlargement of the export surplus. This restates the inconsistency of policy thesis expounded in the *Tract*. Keynes's exposition of the *modus operandi* of bank rate remains a classic of its kind; but it is a price-level, rather than output, adjustment model that he has in mind.

Did Keynes see flexible wages as a complete cure for any shift in the consumption or investment function? One part of the *Treatise* suggests he did. In Book IV, we get a classical credit-cycle story depending on lagged wage adjustment. In the upswing, there is a sequence of commodity (price) inflation, profit inflation, and income inflation, which then reverses itself in the downswing: prices fall, profits fall, and finally money-wages fall as the final act in the adjustment process. Yet in Book III, Keynes tells the famous 'banana parable', in which flexible wages do not cure the initial disturbance because, if intended saving goes up in response to a thrift campaign, while employers reduce wages, 'the spending power of the public will be reduced by just as much as the aggregate costs of production'. If interest rates are fixed, there will be no position of equilibrium till either all production ceases and the community starves to death, or till growing impoverishment causes the community to save less, or unless 'investment is stimulated by some means or another', for example, by loan-financed public works.

If both interest-rate adjustment and public works are ruled out, then the only realistic adjustment mechanism left is impoverishment. Keynes called this 'nature's cure'. He did not make sufficiently clear that the first story (Book IV) related to an open economy in which cost reductions can lead to an increased export demand, and the second to a closed economy in which there is no export sector. He also failed to explain how 'saving' could continue to exceed investment in banana-land in face of cumulative business losses and income decline. This was the main technical business left over from the *Treatise*, largely the result of his non-operational definition of 'saving'.

The main object of national monetary policy should be to maintain a rate of interest consistent with full employment at a price level given, in the long run, by the behaviour of 'efficiency wages'. Such interest-rate autonomy could only be guaranteed by periodic adjustment of the exchange rate. The existence of downward wage rigidity, Keynes argued, was incompatible with a 'laissez-faire attitude to foreign lending'. Hence he doubted whether 'it is wise to have a currency system with a much wider ambit than our banking system, our tariff system and our wage system'. This somewhat extreme statement of monetary nationalism was not entirely inconsistent with the idea of a more flexible international currency system.

Keynes rightly regarded the Fundamental Equations of the *Treatise* as variations on the Fisher and Cambridge equations of exchange. But the causal sequence had been reversed. It was the forces affecting the demand for money balances, not the actions of the monetary authority in supplying those balances, which triggered off changes in the price level. However, he still expected the monetary authority to be able to neutralize the effect of those forces by supplying an appropriate quantity of money. 'Those who attribute sovereign power to the monetary authority in the governance of prices', he wrote,

> do not, of course, claim that the terms on which money is supplied is the *only* influence affecting the price-level. To maintain that the supplies in a reservoir can be maintained at any required level by pouring enough water into it is not inconsistent with admitting that the level of the reservoir depends on many other factors besides how much water is poured in.

Between 1929 and 1931, Keynes used the *Treatise*'s saving—investment disequilibrium model as the basis of his policy advice to Ramsay MacDonald's Labour government, caught up in the first stages of the world depression. On the Macmillan Committee, set up by Philip Snowden, Labour's chancellor of the exchequer, to advise him on currency and credit matters, Keynes put forward six possible remedies for the slump, applicable to Britain's existing position. He ruled out devaluation except as a last resort. There were a number of suggestions for lowering domestic costs of production. One of them, 'an agreed reduction of the level of money incomes', reverted to his suggestion of 1925. Export industries might be relieved of taxes like national insurance contributions; or they might be rationalized. Three further remedies were directed to increasing employment at existing costs of production. The first was Protection, which 'does the trick, whereas in present conditions free trade does not'. The second was his old policy of mobilizing savings running to waste abroad in a loan-financed public works programme. His final remedy was for concerted international action to raise the world price level.

This litany of suggestions was put forward in February–March 1930. Protection became increasingly appealing as the world slump deepened. Keynes had been appointed to the prime minister's new Economic Advisory Council in January 1930; in July, he was made chairman of a subcommittee of economists to produce 'an agreed diagnosis ... and a reasoned list of possible remedies'. In his own memorandum to the committee, dated 21 September 1930, Keynes invented an elegant language for talking about the relationship between Britain's rigid economic structure and its declining international position. He defined the 'equilibrium terms of trade' as those which prevail 'when the level of money wages at home relatively to money wages abroad is such that the amount of the foreign balance (i.e. of foreign investment) *plus* the amount of home investment at the rate of interest set by world conditions ... is ... equal to the amount of home savings'. British unemployment was largely due to the equilibrium terms of trade having been worsened by the return to gold in 1925 without any corresponding reduction in the money costs of production. Sterling's overvaluation had narrowed the export surplus available for foreign investment while imposing a high bank rate, which lowered domestic investment. Thus total investment was falling short of full-employment saving – whence business losses and unemployment.

The policy alternatives suggested by this analysis were to *meet* the worsened equilibrium terms of trade by cutting costs of production (particularly money-wages) or to *improve* them by reducing the pressure to lend abroad and/or enlarging the foreign balance at given terms of trade – pointing to a mixture of loan-financed public investment and protection. Keynes accepted that Britain's standard of living had to fall, but argued that raising prices was a better method for achieving this than lowering money-wages: there would be less social resistance, and the burden would fall on the whole community, including the *rentier* class.

In arguing the case for loan-financed public investment, Keynes made use, for the first time, of a primitive version of Richard Kahn's multiplier theory. Tariff protection was put forward as a way of increasing the foreign balance as well as business confidence, but also because 'any manufacturing country is probably just about as well fitted as any other to manufacture the great majority of articles'. The last sentiment was a fundamental breach with free-trade thinking. If the government rejected such policies, it would logically be forced to meet the equilibrium terms of trade by making deflation effective. The worst policy of all was wobbling between the two.

The exclusion of devaluation and the importance of business 'confidence' thus led Keynes to a theoretically based argument for protection as his favourite 'remedy' for the slump in the period leading up to Britain's abandonment of the gold standard in September 1931. In reaching this politically conservative, if theoretically radical, conclusion, Keynes had been shaken by the evidence of both the Bank of England and the Treasury to the Macmillan Committee earlier that year. The Bank of England had cast doubts on Keynes's belief in the sovereign efficacy of monetary policy. Low interest rates, the Bank's spokesmen had argued, were not enough to make businessmen borrow if investment prospects were gloomy: one could lead the horse to the water, but not make it drink. A loan-financed public works programme, argued Sir Richard Hopkins of the Treasury, would produce 'psychological' crowding out of private investment if there was widespread mistrust of the schemes on which the proceeds of the loan were to be spent – or, he might have added, of the government doing the spending. Protection was the only policy which promised to meet the theoretical *and* confidence requirements of success in the given conditions.

These considerations influenced the subsequent development of Keynes's theory, and indeed of the Keynesian revolution in policy-making. Inventing theoretical models 'relevant' to the real world implied the development of policy instruments appropriate to a wide variety of realistic circumstances. Keynes the theoretician and Keynes the policy adviser were never far apart.

Chapter 4
The General Theory

A strong common core of ideas links the *Treatise on Money* with *The General Theory of Employment, Interest, and Money*. The separation of saving and investment plans; the lack of any 'internal efficacious economic process' (in Samuelson's words) to equilibrate them; the stability of consumption and the volatility of investment; the store of value function of money – all these are present in the earlier book. *The General Theory* added a unifying mechanism in the shape of the 'principle of effective demand'. Keynes offered his profession, for the first time, a theory of demand and supply for output as a whole; he showed that if demand falls short of supply, output may have to run down to bring them back into balance; hence the possibility that 'the economic system may find itself in stable equilibrium ... at a level below full employment'. For economists who wanted to make the world better this was *the* crucial breakthrough. It explained the slump and showed how an escape from it might be consciously organized.

As Keynes put it, the new book switched attention from the analysis of the *causes* of a change in the level of output to the analysis of the *effects* of a change in the level of output – something which had been left 'incomplete and extremely confused' in the earlier book. This is the nearest Keynes got to saying that both books are needed to understand the *Gestalt* of modern economies. In practice, the *Treatise* was forgotten and *The General Theory* became the bible of the economics profession and the politicians they advised.

Whether, but for the collapse of the world economy, Keynes, or anyone else, would have been thus interested in switching the spotlight from causes to effects is doubtful. What people wanted analysed in the 1930s was not institutional obstacles to the adjustment from one position of satisfactory equilibrium to another, but factors capable of keeping economic activity at a low level. Equally, policy was now required not to dampen oscillations round a full-employment equilibrium – the traditional aim of the monetary reformers – but to raise the equilibrium level of employment. Keynes provided both theory and policy for the new conditions. Psychology and expectations move to the centre of his analytical picture; and he provided new concepts, terms, and tools directly useful to the policy-maker.

Keynes's thinking was directly affected by the world depression in two ways. First, the depression undermined his faith in monetary policy – a radical break from his personal past. Despite the cheap money which followed sterling's depreciation in 1931, recovery was very weak. Keynes concluded that 'direct state intervention to promote and subsidise new investment' might offer the only 'means of escape from prolonged and perhaps interminable depression'.

Secondly, it shifted his attention, more than ever before, from Britain to the United States. The problematic of the *Treatise on Money* was that of a sclerotic economy with an overvalued exchange rate. American wages and prices were much more flexible than those in Britain, its foreign sector much smaller, yet its output collapse was much more dramatic. American events spurred Keynes to think more generally about the predicament of wealthy economies. Moreover, the fact that the slump was worldwide made the search for remedies involving devaluation, protection, or other 'external' elements irrelevant. *The General*

Theory would try to explain how the closing of the investment frontier, combined with a high propensity to save, could make 'involuntary' unemployment endemic in rich Western societies at large. The 'closed economy' model of *The General Theory* and 'fiscal' Keynesianism can both be seen as products of the world slump.

One early technical debate provoked by the *Treatise* was directly influenced by the state of the world. The Fundamental Equations are price-level equations. Changes in output and employment are merely incidents – even if potentially protracted and painful ones – in the adjustment of the cost of producing output to the price at which it can be profitably sold. This analytic picture, taken over from Keynes's earlier *Tract on Monetary Reform*, seemed to fit the slump of 1920–1, when the fall in output and employment appeared to be an induced effect of falling prices. But it was at odds with the slump of 1930–1, whose earliest, most dramatic, and enduring effects in industrial countries were felt on output and employment, not prices.

Even before the *Treatise* was published, Ralph Hawtrey tried to convince Keynes that the causation ran directly from changes in spending to changes in output. 'If anything occurs to affect the demand for goods,' Hawtrey wrote to Keynes in 1930, 'the first result is an increase or decrease in sales *at existing prices* ... There is always some interval of time before prices are adjusted, and the interval may be considerable.' On 28 November 1930, Keynes conceded that price and output changes might both play a part in adjusting an economy to a demand shock, and that 'it will probably be difficult in the future to prevent monetary theory and the theory of short-period supply from running together'. In Keynes's mind, the direct effects of a change in spending on quantities start to overshadow its effects on costs and prices.

The disequilibrium analysis of the *Treatise* posed a different technical problem. How did Keynes suppose the 'excess of saving over investment' to be eliminated if, for some reason or other, the rate of interest was not free to fall? In the banana parable, he suggested that the growing impoverishment of the community would eventually restore equilibrium by reducing the amount it saved. But this shadowy sketch of an income-adjustment mechanism was hampered by the *Treatise* definitions which made the 'excess of saving over investment' identical to business losses. This meant that saving would always 'run ahead' of investment as the economy ran down. Dennis Robertson's criticism of September 1931 was decisive:

> How many of those ... who have taken up the cry that a slump is due to an excess of Saving over Investment realise that the savings which are so deplorably abundant during a slump consist largely of entrepreneurs' incomes which are not being spent, for the simple reason that they have not been earned?

If businessmen's losses were counted as deductions from the national income, the 'excess savings' disappeared.

In a note of 22 March 1932, Keynes 'bowed the knee' to Robertson (as well as to Hawtrey and Hayek) by proposing a definition of 'total income' to include 'abnormal' profits and losses, so that 'savings and investment are, necessarily and at all times, equal'. Further 'S[aving out of total income] always and necessarily accommodates itself to I[nvestment] ... [It] is no longer the dog ... but the tail'. Thus by 2 May 1932, Keynes can say that 'the volume of employment depends on the amount of investment, and ... anything which increases or decreases the latter will increase or decrease the former'.

From the wreck of the *Treatise*'s special definitions the fundamental units of Keynes's *General Theory* – consumption, investment, income, output – are starting to emerge. These would lend themselves to statistical measurement, hence to national income accounting, hence to precise policy targets.

'Gentlemen, the change in title of these lectures' – from 'The Pure Theory of Money' to 'The Monetary Theory of Production' – 'is significant'. With these words on 10 October 1932, recalled Lorie Tarshis, 'Keynes began the first of his eight lectures and in effect announced the beginning of the Keynesian Revolution'. The subject of Keynes's enquiry was: what determines the volume of output in a monetary economy? The question is *The General Theory*'s, but much of the answer is still wrapped up in the language and concepts of the *Treatise on Money*. Nevertheless, many of the familiar building-blocks of *The General Theory* are in view. They are even clearer in the repeat set of lectures he delivered in the autumn of 1933.

The volume of output is determined by aggregate 'disbursement', or expenditure. If spending on current output falls short of current income – if, in the language of the *Treatise*, the sales proceeds from current output fall short of the costs of producing it – income has to fall to the level of expenditure, via a reduction in output and employment. In explaining why the costs of production can be reduced only by cutting employment rather than by cutting money-wages, Keynes offers a first sketch of chapter 2 of *The General Theory*. The argument is sharpened in 1933 by the proposition that the real wage depends on the state of effective demand, not on the money-wage bargain ('there may be no escape for labour from high real wages in a slump') and by the corresponding concept of 'involuntary unemployment'. In the absence of the possibility of real wage adjustment, the classical theory's reliance on Say's Law – 'supply creates its own demand' – for the continuous maintenance of full employment is also asserted.

Expenditure is determined, in a *laissez-faire* economy, by the 'factors of market psychology': the state of time preference (later the consumption function) relating saving to income; expected 'quasi-rents' or the expected profitability of investment (later the marginal efficiency of capital); and the state of liquidity preference, which, together with the quantity of money, determines the rate of interest. These 'parameters' of a monetary economy, together with the aggregate supply schedule and 'earnings response' (of costs to prices) tell us 'what state of output would ensue . . . and how the parameters would have to be influenced to get the desired output'. This is put more sharply in 1933: 'the fundamental forces determining the volume of employment are the state of confidence, the propensity to consume, liquidity preference and the quantity of money. We may call this the General Law of Employment.' The role of expectations and uncertainty are now much more prominently highlighted.

That the amount of aggregate disbursement determined by the 'factors of psychology' may be insufficient to maintain a full employment volume of output is clear to Keynes but the reason is not precisely stated in 1932. Keynes has already decided that the rate of interest is determined by the demand for money, rather than by the demand for loans. So decided, the interest rate 'fixes the present value of the prospective quasi-rents'. But there is no clear statement of his later doctrine that the validity of Say's Law depends on the efficacy of the classical interest-rate adjustment mechanism. Rather, he sticks to the *Treatise* doctrine that the monetary authority has complete control over the short and long rates, its duty being to 'maintain a rate of interest which leads to an optimum level of investment'. The proposition that the 'speculative' motive for holding money may set a floor to the fall in the interest rate is not clearly stated till 1933.

Keynes asks: what, in the absence of stabilization policy, is to stop income and output running down 'until production was at a total standstill?' The short answer is that, following a shock to investment, expenditure (consumption) falls less than income. It is this which makes possible 'stable equilibrium'. This, too, is said more sharply in 1933: 'Saving must equal Investment, income will adjust itself to meet this condition.' From any low level, income cannot be increased unless the 'propensity to save' is reduced or the amount of investment is increased. The advantage of Keynes's less precise formulation of 1932 is that it retains the cyclical analysis of the *Treatise*. The slump in income will tend to bring about a fall in interest rates as the ratio of money stock to income rises, allowing increased investment. But unless the interest rate is deliberately lowered further by banking policy, the 'increase in investment . . . may not be as rapid as the increase in savings as output begins to rise again', leaving the recovery to peter out before full employment is reached. This gives a more complete idea of Keynes's notion of subnormal 'equilibrium' than he managed in *The General Theory*, whose static analysis was designed to fix the economy at a point in time in order to give policy a precise target to aim at.

One reason for the relative imprecision of the 1932 lectures is that Keynes made no use of Kahn's multiplier theory. Like Kahn himself, he failed to see its logical connection with monetary equilibrium analysis.

Richard Kahn's article, 'The Relation of Home Investment to Unemployment', published in the *Economic Journal* in June 1931, was designed to combat the British Treasury's objections to loan-financed public works programmes as a remedy for unemployment. These were based on the meagreness of the employment afforded by a given expenditure of money, the budgetary burden entailed, and the 'crowding out' of private investment. In their pamphlet of 1929, *Can Lloyd George Do It?* Keynes and Henderson had asserted that a public works programme would provide, in addition to a calculable amount of primary employment, 'secondary' employment resulting from the newly employed spending their wages, but that these secondary effects were incalculable. The question Kahn asked was: what was to stop an extra £1 of income in one person's hands from raising the community's income to infinity? The intuitive answer is that some fraction of the extra income will be 'saved' each time it is spent until the stimulus exhausts itself. Provided this fraction is known, the total of increased income or secondary employment can be summed to a finite number, which can be expressed as a ratio or multiple either of the initial investment or of primary employment. Moreover, the additional investment would, by raising aggregate incomes, create an equivalent amount of saving, thus exemplifying Keynes's assertion that 'investment always drags saving along with it at an equal pace', and countering the Treasury argument that loan-financed public investment would take savings from existing uses. This in essence is the multiplier theory.

It was not how Kahn set it out. He achieved his 'leakages' from the enlarged expenditure stream by deducting unemployment benefit (what the unemployed were already spending) and extra spending on imports (which did not directly increase domestic employment); and he failed to realize that his formula had established the necessary equality between saving and investment. (In an 'open' economy, the necessary equality is not between saving and investment but between saving and imports and investment and exports.) The *personal* saving leakage first entered the multiplier literature with an article by the Danish statistician Jens Warming in the *Economic Journal* of June 1932. Warming 'combined an exclusively income-related personal saving function with Kahn's own multiplier algebra to render neatly the income adjustment mechanism by which saving is equilibrated with an initiating change in investment'. Keynes almost certainly saw Warming's article when it was first submitted to the *Economic Journal*. So the theoretical influence may have run more directly from Warming to Keynes than from Kahn to Keynes at this point. Kahn, influenced in turn by Warming, presented a multiplier derived from the marginal propensities to save and import in a paper in Cincinatti, USA, in December 1932. Keynes's *The Means to Prosperity*, published three months later, presented this revised version of Kahn's theory in support of his argument for a loan-financed public works programme.

The multiplier is the most notorious piece of Keynesian magic. It abstracted from the confidence ('crowding out') issue and from the budget-funding problem. The precision of the employment, as opposed to the income, multiplier was always something of a confidence trick, depending on an arbitrary assumption as to how the increased spending would be split between higher production and higher prices. This did not matter much in the early 1930s when prices were falling, but it was to have baleful effects after the war. Many Keynesians would assert baldly that 'quantities adjust, not prices'. Keynes's own famous mistrust of the notion of a 'calculable future' fell victim in this case to his passionate urge to give governments tools of action.

Much ink has been spilt over the question of when exactly Keynes came to understand his new theory of effective demand. That it was some time between 1932 and 1933 is indisputable. Beyond that it depends on the test of understanding being used. Perhaps Keynes himself should have the last word, though this is too much to be hoped for. Original thinking, he remarked in his lecture of 6 November 1933, starts as a 'grey; fuzzy, woolly monster' in one's head. 'The precise use of language comes at a late stage in the development of one's thoughts. You can think accurately and effectively long before you can, so to speak, photograph your thought.' Keynes knew more than he could say in the autumn of 1932, but he was more confident about what he knew a year later, and therefore could say it better.

The General Theory of Employment, Interest, and Money, published on 4 February 1936, is a work of enduring fascination. It is simple and subtle, obscure and profound. It offered a systematic way of thinking not just about behaviour of contemporary economies, but about the pitfalls in the quest for greater wealth at all times. It combined a vision of how economies behave with a rigorous demonstration of the possibility of underemployment equilibrium. Although young economists of speculative bent were drawn to it as a storehouse of suggestive ideas, it was its practical usefulness which chiefly attracted them in a world poised between a decaying democracy and rampaging totalitarianism.

It is by no means as badly organized as it is often held to be. The reader who starts with chapter 3 and then reads chapters 8–13, and chapter 18 can get an accurate idea of the core of Keynes's theory. The main problems arise when Keynes tries to relate his own theory to what he calls 'classical theory', by way of comment, attempted reconciliation, or, more usually, destructive criticism. The difficulties are particularly acute in chapter 2, 'Postulates of Classical Economics', chapters 14 and 15, which deal with the classical theory of the rate of interest and the more complete statement of his own theory of interest, and in Book V on 'Money-Wages and Prices'. Chapter 16, 'Sundry Observations on the Nature of Capital', and chapter 17, 'The Essential Properties of Interest and Money', as well as Book VI (chapters 22–4), are best read as general thoughts, speculative and visionary, arising from the core theory. Book II, 'Definitions and Ideas' (chapters 4–7), can be, and usually is, skipped.

In *The General Theory*, Keynes used a Marshallian 'short-period' analysis. The capital stock is fixed, so that the only way the economy can adjust to a demand shock is by a more or less intensive use of existing plant. This seemed a reasonable analytic device in the circumstances of the Great Depression. But it excluded changes in the 'structure of production' which the Austrian and Swedish economists regarded as central to the adjustment process, whether or not it was accompanied by unemployment.

Another characteristic of Keynes's analytical method should be noted. He abjures Walrasian-type general equilibrium reasoning in favour of a logical chain of causation. Typical from *The General Theory* is the following sequence: given the propensity to consume, the amount of employment is determined by the amount of investment; given the expected profitability of investment, the amount of investment is determined by the rate of interest; given the quantity of money, the rate of interest is determined by liquidity preference. This causal chain, as we shall see, is used to demonstrate that if the income (sales proceeds) which entrepreneurs expect from employing n people is expected to fall below the costs of employing that number, then output and employment will fall till the costs of employment equal expected sales proceeds.

Keynes rearranges the 'classical' view that 'involuntary' unemployment is impossible into the same kind of chain logic in order to emphasize its dependence on the classical theory of the rate of interest. Given the real wage, the level of employment depends on Say's Law that 'supply creates its own demand'; given the expected profitability of investment, Say's Law depends on the rate of interest being wholly determined in the market for loans. If this is untrue, the classical theory falls to the ground.

Three points need to be made about Keynes's definitions (Book II) before we get into the main argument. First, saving and investment are equal by definition, according to the equations: Income = Consumption + Investment; Saving = Income − Consumption; therefore Saving = Investment. This raises the question: what has to adjust in the economy to validate the last equation? Secondly, Keynes proposed to deflate changes in nominal income by wage rates – money payments per hour worked – in order to measure the employment impact of a change in demand. Given the average wage rate, employment will change by the same amount as nominal income. This seemed a reasonable short-period simplification, but it begged the question how adjustment is shared between employment and wages in actual situations. Finally, by making short-period employment depend mainly on expectations of long-period profit, Keynes introduced the 'method of expectations' into the determination of short-period equilibrium.

The General Theory makes explicit an idea that is only implicit in Keynes's previous two books: that money is not just a medium of exchange but a store of wealth. The necessary condition for this function of money is uncertainty: holding it reduces exposure to risk and thus alleviates anxiety. It is rather unfortunate that it was not till p. 168 that Keynes introduced the 'demand for money' into his 'causal nexus', since all his conclusions, indeed the *raison d'être* of *The General Theory*, flow from his perception that, when uncertainty becomes too great, liquidity provides a retreat from activity. The entrepreneur always faces a choice between using money in this way or in some other way *or not using it at all*. People's freedom not to spend in a monetary economy is thus the logical crux of Keynes's denial that 'supply creates its own demand'. Instead, 'expenditure creates its own income'. These thoughts underlie his 'vision'.

Books III and IV, dealing with consumption demand, investment demand, and the rate of interest, are the analytical kernel of Keynes's book, because these variables are what determine the volume of output and the level of employment. In the short run, the 'propensity to consume' (and therefore to save) is a 'fairly stable' proportion of current income. The shape of the function (what fraction of increasing or decreasing income is saved) enables one to sum (via the multiplier) to a finite number the amount of income adjustment needed to equilibrate saving and investment plans. The consumption function enables Keynes to explain why, following a demand shock, income and output do not run down forever (as in banana-land) but issue in a position of 'underemployment equilibrium', and tells governments how much extra they need to spend to eliminate the 'output gap'. Together with the investment multiplier, it is the most useful policy tool bequeathed by *The General Theory*.

It is important to notice that, while *realized* saving and investment are equal by definition, *planned* saving and investment need not be. When they are not, some plans at least will be either exceeded or disappointed. An excess of planned saving over planned investment sets up contractionary forces; an excess of planned investment over planned saving sets up expansionary ones.

In all this, Keynes stands the classical psychology on its head. The classical economists praised 'parsimony' or 'thrift' as increasing the supply of capital. Keynes's 'paradox of thrift' was that an increase in intended saving was liable to lead to a reduction in actual saving, via a fall in income, unless the expected profitability of investment was going up independently. But an increased propensity to save was liable to have exactly the opposite effect on investment by reducing entrepreneurs' expectation of future consumption on which the profitability of investment depends. Moreover, in so far as the marginal propensity to save was likely to rise with income, the problem of securing an adequate amount of investment tended to worsen over time. To maintain full employment a rich society will need to invest an increasing proportion of its income even as the expected profitability of investment declines, as the gap between income and consumption widens.

Given the 'propensity to consume', the amount of employment depends on the rate of investment, or additions to capital stock. There is an 'inducement to invest' when the expected return on the investment is higher than the cost of undertaking it: when what Keynes calls the 'marginal efficiency of capital' is positive. In chapter 12, 'The State of Long-Term Expectations', the instability of investment demand emerges as the crucial cause of economic fluctuations. The reason is the volatility attaching to expectations of the future yield of investment.

Keynes's starting-point is the 'extreme precariousness of the basis of knowledge on which our estimates of prospective yield have to be made'. The stock exchange reduces the riskiness of investments by making them 'liquid' for individuals, but this makes investment as a whole much more volatile, since investors can buy and sell at a moment's notice. Share prices depend not on real investment prospects, which are largely unknowable, but on prevailing sentiment, which can fluctuate violently with the day's news. It is the flimsiness of knowledge supporting conventional share valuations which makes the investment function peculiarly dependent on 'animal spirits', defined as 'a spontaneous urge to action rather than inaction'.

Many Keynesians have seen chapter 12 as containing the 'vision' of *The General Theory*, and indeed of the Keynesian revolution, both in its attack on the ethics of capitalism – 'when the capital development of a country becomes a by-product of the activities of a casino, the job is likely to be ill-done' – and in its rejection of calculability in human affairs. The discussion leads naturally to the conclusion that the state should take 'an ever greater responsibility for directly organizing investment . . . on long views'. It also establishes the rationality of liquidity preference – a preference for holding cash rather than investing it – which plays a central part in Keynes's theory of the rate of interest.

Given the state of expectations, the amount of investment is determined by the rate of interest. Keynes's belief is that the rate of interest is determined in the market for money. He takes interest to be the price for giving up liquidity – instant command over sums of money. It is, he was to say in 1937, 'the measure of the degree of our disquietude'. The greater people's preference for holding their savings in money, the higher the rate of interest people will demand for parting with money. The chain of logic of *The General Theory* is thus completed by showing that the rate of interest can remain above the 'rate of return to capital' necessary to secure full employment.

The 'necessary condition', indeed the 'sole intelligible explanation' of the existence of liquidity preference is 'the existence of *uncertainty* as to the future of the rate of interest'. Keynes reasons that, if this were not so, investors who wanted to get out of equities would buy government debt. This would drive up the price of bonds and lower their yield, making it more profitable for businessmen to borrow for investment. But if speculators think the interest rate is 'too low' – has fallen below its 'conventional' or expected level – they will sell bonds for cash, thus aborting, or reversing, the fall in the rate. Keynes does not enquire into what causes the expected rate of interest to be what it is – a point which Dennis Robertson was to pick up.

The monetary authority can step in by buying bonds itself (open-market operations). But this can generate offsetting bond sales by the private sector if monetary policy is regarded as 'unsound'. One can then get a 'liquidity trap', a situation when monetary policy cannot push the interest rate beneath a floor set by the fear of inflation or default. The lower the rate of interest the smaller the 'earnings from illiquidity' available to insure against risk of loss on capital account. This, says Keynes, is the main obstacle to the fall of the interest rate to a very low figure. A long-term interest rate of 2% 'leaves more to fear than to hope, and offers, at the same time, a running yield which is only sufficient to offset a very small measure of fear'. Liquidity preference may then become 'virtually absolute' in that almost everyone prefers holding cash to holding a debt. However, the flight into cash might occur at a higher rate of interest, as in the United States in 1932. In this event, the monetary authority will have lost effective control over the long rate. However, a monetary policy in which the public has confidence may succeed where one judged 'experimental in character or easily liable to change' will fail.

Keynes's discussion of the interest-rate problem goes to the heart of his theory. His assertion that liquidity preference may keep the interest rate too high for a full-employment level of investment clinches, in his view, his theoretical assault on the doctrine that 'supply creates its own demand'. The rejection of the idea that interest is a reward for saving undermines the classical idea that thriftiness is a virtue in a depression, since it does not lower the interest rate and thus encourage investment. The possible inefficacy of monetary policy to assure the same result reinforces the case for fiscal policy in combating depression.

This concludes the positive part of Keynes's 'general theory'. The basic ideas are 'extremely simple', as he said in his preface. The real difficulties arise in understanding not so much his own theory but its relationship to what he called 'classical' theory. To what extent was it inconsistent with received doctrine? And if inconsistent, to what extent was it a 'truer', or as Keynes put it, a more 'general' theory? To neither of these questions is a conclusive answer possible. Keynes set up his own theory against his own version of 'classical' theory, which many of his opponents denied holding. Also it is not very clear what he meant by 'general'. In the book's first chapter, he contrasted it with the 'special case assumed by the classical theory'; elsewhere he contrasted it with 'partial', as when he attacks the classical theory for ignoring the interdependencies between the labour and goods markets.

Keynes opened his account by attacking the 'classical' view that employment is determined in the labour market. Basing himself on Pigou's *Theory of Unemployment* (1933), he argued in chapter 2 that the classical theorists believed that, with perfect money-wage flexibility, there was no obstacle to full employment, whatever the state of nominal demand.

In the 'classical' account, as Keynes depicted it, the amount of employment depends on two 'real' wage 'postulates': that, in equilibrium, the wage equals the marginal product of labour, and that it is equal to the marginal disutility of labour. The first gives a downward-sloping demand curve for labour, which reflects the decreasing marginal efficiency of work; the second gives an upward-sloping supply curve, reflecting the increasing marginal disutility or 'pain' of work. With perfectly flexible wages, the amount of employment is determined at the point where the real disutility suffered (and wage paid) for the last hour worked just equals the value of what it is worth in revenue to the employer, i.e.

there is no obstacle to continuous full employment. In such a world, there can be no involuntary unemployment, only voluntarily chosen leisure together with some 'frictional' unemployment. The leisure was voluntary because workers could always escape from it by revising their psychic computations of pain and pleasure, and accepting whatever was available to them for additional work. (It was never obvious how notions of diminishing efficiency and pleasure attached to 'hours' of work could be translated into quantities of employment in a weekly waged system. The usual solution was to assume that increasing employment absorbed workers of decreasing quality and increasing leisure-preference.)

Keynes accepted the first, but rejected the second classical postulate. He thought that circumstances could arise in which more workers were willing to work at whatever *money*-wage was 'going' than the amount of jobs being offered. Labour as a whole would be off its supply curve: hence 'involuntary unemployment'. The reason was that wage bargains were made in money. If, following a negative shock to demand, wages and prices immediately fell together, the real wage would remain the same. Nothing would have happened to improve business prospects, so unemployment would still develop. Pigou argued that, with perfect wage flexibility, wages would fall more than employers' incomes (profits) – costs more than prices – reducing the real wage and allowing more employment. Keynes turned this argument neatly round by putting 'expected' in front of 'incomes'. The effect of a fall in money-wages on employment would depend on what it did for profit expectations. As he had put it neatly in 1933: 'Income is the expectation that induces [entrepreneurs] to do what [they] are doing.'

Here the argument in chapter 2 was broken off to be resumed in Book V, after Keynes had explained his own theory. In chapter 19, 'Changes in Money-Wages', Keynes considers the effect of money-wage reductions on the determinants of aggregate demand: investment, saving, and liquidity preference. His main conclusion is that an all-round reduction in money-wages *can* indirectly improve employment in a closed system, on two conditions: (*a*) if falling wages improve business confidence, and (*b*) by leading to a reduction in the price level and hence in the demand for transaction balances relative to the stock of money, allowing a fall in the interest rate. But a surer policy for achieving (*b*) would be to increase the nominal stock of money: 'only . . . a foolish person . . . would prefer a flexible wage policy to a flexible money policy'. As he had put it in chapter 2: involuntary unemployment exists when a rise in prices relative to wage rates would increase the quantity of employment.

In his review of *The General Theory*, David Champernowne attached a condition to Keynes's employment-raising policy: it would work only if employed workers refrained from demanding a higher money-wage in response to a rise in prices. He predicted that their acceptance of a real wage reduction would be undermined by inflation, as unfortunately turned out in the end to be the case. This has led to the frequent charge that Keynes's methods of increasing employment depend on 'money illusion' – lowering the value of money and hoping that workers would not notice that their real wage had gone down. The charge is unfair. Keynes was merely echoing the prevalent belief that a recovery from depression required the *recovery* of prices to their pre-depression or 'normal' level. He assumed, that is, a continuation of a stationary cost of living, with wage-earners not adjusting their contracts to hold on to temporary windfalls. He was not suggesting pumping more money into an economy already subject to inflationary pressure.

In chapter 21, 'The Theory of Prices', Keynes acknowledges that rising employment will be accompanied by moderately rising prices, apart from any change in average wage rates, because labour is not homogeneous, because there are likely to be supply 'bottle-necks', and because the cost of capital might rise faster than the cost of labour. Indeed, such a rise in the price level relative to wage rates was accepted by Keynes as a necessary condition of increased employment, as we have seen. But, in addition, recovery is likely to put upward pressure on money-wages. Thus, there are likely to be positions of 'semi-inflation' short of full employment. At full employment, the quantity theory of money comes into its own, any further increase in money demand going wholly into raising prices. Chapter 21 makes it clear that the conventional summary of *The General Theory*'s message, 'quantities adjust, not prices', is seriously incomplete. Indeed, chapter 21 leaves indeterminate how the increase (or for that matter decrease) in money demand is divided between prices, wages, and output, though Keynes thinks it reasonable to assume that 'a moderate [increase] in effective demand, coming on a situation where there is widespread unemployment, may spend itself very little in raising prices and mainly in increasing employment'. In 1939, he was half-persuaded by J. G. Dunlop and L. Tarshis that increasing returns and imperfect competition would lower average unit costs as employment increased, obviating the need for prices to rise and real wages to fall; and many post-war Keynesians thought that this factor would be sufficient to rob full-employment policies of any inflationary danger. That was the real illusion.

The upshot of Keynes's discussion of the wages problem was to knock on the head the 'classical' contention, that, with money-wage rates perfectly flexible, there is no obstacle to full employment at any level of money income. Rather, Keynes showed that only one level of money income (or aggregate demand) will bring about a real wage consistent with full employment, i.e. that over a wide range of actual circumstances the real wage was determined not in the labour market but by the whole range of factors influencing the level of demand for goods in the economy.

How important is Keynes's rate-of-interest theory in his denial of Say's Law? The consumption function/multiplier mechanism seems sufficient to explain the process of income adjustment. Consumption is strictly a function of income; the multiplier tells you how much income will have to change to equilibrate saving and investment plans. If the further assumption is made that investment is not sensitive to small interest changes, then the interest rate is not actually needed to explain anything: as Keynes said, it was left 'hanging in the air'. But, as a concession to Roy Harrod, Keynes had agreed to include a diagram, which showed saving as a function of interest as well as income. Thus the rate of interest was needed to establish a 'determinate equilibrium'. Consumption-function Keynesians have always regretted this concession to Harrod, because it seems to make the theoretical relevance of *The General Theory* depend on the existence of liquidity preference. If one could then show that Keynes had exaggerated the pervasiveness of liquidity preference, or that it did not provide a complete theory of interest, the way was open to make some damaging attacks on Keynes's theoretical structure.

Keynes's erstwhile collaborator, Dennis Robertson, concentrated on the second of these points. He pointed out that to say that the rate of interest is a function of the 'speculative' demand for money does not provide a complete theory of interest, because a fall in the transactions demand for money relative to the money stock will reduce the rate of interest and promote investment (something Keynes had admitted). Robertson claimed that this re-established the classical loanable-funds theory of the rate of interest related to the underlying forces of 'productivity and thrift'. It explained the observed fact that interest rates fell in a slump and rose in a boom. A testy series of articles and rejoinders in the *Economic Journal* followed, which ended with Keynes proposing to print a note which contained the words, 'I hear with surprise [from Robertson] that our forebears believed that . . . an increase in the desire to save would lead to a recession in employment and income and would only result in a fall in the rate of interest in so far as this was the case.' He wrote to Robertson on 25 July 1938: 'Our forebears believed that . . . the rate of interest depends on the supply of saving. My theory is that it depends on the supply of inactive money. There is no possible reconcilation between these views.'

Keynes's other eminent Cambridge colleague and principal stalking-horse of *The General Theory*, Arthur Pigou, attacked Keynes from a different standpoint. Pigou claimed, in the *Economic Journal* of December 1943, that a deficiency in aggregate demand would lead to lower prices, thus increasing the real value of cash balances and hence net wealth in so far as such balances were unmatched by debts. This 'Pigou effect' increases consumption, raising aggregate demand back eventually to its long-run full-employment level.

Robertson and Pigou were fighting a rearguard action to show not that the classical scheme of thought denied the possibility of 'involuntary unemployment', but that such unemployment could not be part of an equilibrium state. The decline in the economy set in motion forces of recovery, irrespective of the policy of the monetary authority. However, though the existence of these forces was later admitted, and Keynes's assault on the classical theory judged to be logically flawed, orthodox theory was not thereby rehabilitated. Keynes's critics were forced to concede that recovery forces came into play uncertainly and feebly after a long period of subnormal activity; and they were thus of little interest to economists or governments who believed that Keynes had given them the tools to prevent large-scale fluctuations in demand from occurring in the first place, or reversing them quickly when they did occur.

Much of the rest of *The General Theory* is intended to be suggestive rather than conclusive. It contains a theory of economic history, in which the weakness of the 'inducement of invest', owing to uncertainty, is presented as a permanent problem, and in which the 19th century is seen as a 'special case' in which the psychological propensities are in such a relation as to establish 'a reasonably satisfactory average level of employment'. There are the 'Notes on Mercantilism' in chapter 23 in which Keynes tries to establish a historical lineage for his concern with effective demand, in contrast to mainstream economic thinking based on Ricardo, which supposes that economics is the study of how given resources are allocated among different uses. There are what Pigou called his 'Day of Judgment' reflections on the fate of mature capitalist economies if the state is not brought in to supplement failing private investment demand. One version of the 'secular stagnation' thesis, in chapter 17, 'The Essential Properties of Interest and Money', has particularly fascinated some economists. In this superb crystallization of his deflationary vision, Keynes suggests that the desire to accumulate money can knock out all other forms of production, so that wealthy societies, like King Midas, drown in a sea of gold. After the war, governments succeeded in making money 'go bad', with consequences that Keynes – in another frame of mind – predicted in 1933: 'an entrepreneurial system which would be as prone to excessive demand and over-employment, as our actual system is to deficient demand and under-employment'.

Keynes's last chapter, 'Concluding Notes on Social Philosophy', may be seen as an updating of his Middle Way ideas of the 1920s, suggested by his new theory. Excessive thriftiness could be tackled by redistributing spending power to those with a high propensity to consume (the workers) and by reducing the rewards of thriftiness by fixing a low interest rate. This would remove the scope for savers to live off the scarcity value of capital: 'the euthanasia of the *rentier*' would be the consequence. Because banking policy was unlikely to be able to maintain an 'optimum rate of interest', Keynes advocated 'a somewhat comprehensive socialisation of investment', an ambiguous phrase which has to be interpreted in the light of his endorsement ten years previously of the growth of the public utility sector of the economy (see above pp. 44–5). With demand deficiency removed, Fascism and Communism would lose their appeal, and the full benefits and promise of the 'Manchester system' realized: efficiency and freedom and variety of life at home, mutual harmony and peace abroad. In a much-quoted peroration, Keynes anticipated his intellectual triumph by writing that 'the power of vested interests is vastly exaggerated compared with the gradual encroachment of ideas'.

Keynes did not have to wait long. The intellectual conversion of all the younger British and American economists started soon after *The General Theory* was published, Keynesian fiscal policy began to be used in 1940 in the United States and in 1941 in Britain.

What was accepted was by no means all Keynes had bequeathed. It was the English economist John Hicks, a newcomer to the Keynesian revolution, who in 1937 produced the 'portable' Keynesian model, which has been studied by economics students ever since. In essence, Hicks transforms Keynes's chain logic into a set of simultaneous equations which he depicts diagrammatically by means of his famous IS/LM curves. This 'generalized' system has room for Keynes's 'special theory' – in which saving is determined by income, investment is relatively interest-inelastic, and liquidity preference rules interest rates – but also for at least some versions of the 'Treasury View' which Keynes wrote *The General Theory* to refute. It all depends on the slopes of the curves. Keynes's theory and the classical theory emerge as 'special cases' of the true 'general theory', with Keynes's special case assumed to be the most useful for policy. Hicks's was an astonishing performance.

Keynes, who, above all, sought to influence policy, did not resist this reconciling way of selling his ideas if it made them more accessible and acceptable to the younger economists. But he took advantage of the controversy which followed *The General Theory*'s publication to restate his theory in 1937 in a way which brought out better than his book had its epistemic assumptions. For the 'fundamentalist' Keynesians this article of 1937 in the *Quarterly Journal of Economics* is the canonical statement of the Master's position.

Keynes's restatement of the 'essence' of *The General Theory* is concerned particularly with the effects of uncertainty on investment and the rate of interest: it draws out from the book, that is, the argument of chapter 12, 'The State of Long-Term Expectations', which emphasizes the volatility of investment demand, and those of chapters 13 and 17, which explain why liquidity, or money, carries a premium. It is, above all, the desire for liquidity which makes a decentralized enterpreneurial economy unstable and ensures that its oscillations normally occur round a subnormal level of activity. Why, Keynes asks, should anyone outside a lunatic asylum wish to use money as a store of wealth? The only intelligible answer is the existence of radical uncertainty – a possibility assumed away by the classical assumption of a 'definite and calculable future'. In the article of 1937, there is no consumption function, no investment multiplier, only vague and uncertain knowledge, fluctuating states of confidence, and courage, fears, and hopes, coped with, as best they can be, by strategies and conventions, themselves liable to be swept away by changes in the 'news'. Uncertainty, Keynes suggests, is the human condition. That is why *The General Theory* retains, in Shackle's words, the 'quality of imperishable relevance to the ... insoluble problems of time-bound humanity'.

In this final distillation of his thought, money, or what Keynes calls liquidity, emerges, above all, as a strategy for calming the nerves. Technically, he had come a long way since his early days as monetary reformer, but his vision had not changed much. His whole work, like that of his entire generation of economists, revolved round the unruliness of money, its awesome power to disturb the real economy. They all wanted to make the monetary economy behave like a 'real exchange' economy – one in which there was no unemployment. The deepest question posed by Keynes's work is as follows. Is it money which causes the economy to misbehave? Or is it uncertainty which causes money to misbehave? Between these two views the theory of monetary policy is still poised.

Chapter 5
Economic statesmanship

Keynes was as creative in administration as he was in theory. For every economic problem which interested him he had ready a 'Keynes Plan', drafted at lightning speed. The common feature of these plans – which go back to his proposal for an Indian Central Bank in 1913, praised by Marshall as a 'prodigy of constructive work' – is that while always ahead of the intellectual orthodoxy of the moment they could be readily fitted to existing administrative arrangements. Keynes could thus present them as evolutionary developments of existing practice. The partial exception is his endorsement of a centrally directed public works programme in 1929, which would have required a revolution in government. But this was a Lloyd George, not a Keynes, plan; Keynes's own preference was to channel increased investment through the public utility corporations. He also favoured indirect (financial) to direct (physical) control over the economy, in order to retain the advantages of decentralized decision-making. This brought him into conflict with socialist methods, if not with some aspects of the socialist ideal.

The outbreak of war with Germany on 3 September 1939 posed the kind of economic challenge he could not shirk; and he responded with two articles, 'Paying for the War', published in *The Times*, on 14 and 15 November, and recast and expanded into a booklet, *How to Pay for the War*, which appeared in February 1940, five months before his return to the Treasury. *How to Pay for the War* has been hailed as the first major application to policy of *The General Theory* model of the economy, and so it was. But it also reflected Keynes's experience as a Treasury official in the First World War.

With full employment assured through the big increase in state orders, the problem Keynes faced in 1939 was to transfer resources to the war effort without undue inflation, disincentive tax levels, or the bureaucratic controls associated with comprehensive physical planning. In the First World War, increased government purchases had caused prices to rise; rising prices had reduced the real incomes of the working class; the 'windfall' profits of entrepreneurs were commandeered by the government in the form of taxes and loans. The results were industrial unrest in the later stages of the war; a high cost of government borrowing, which increased the post-war debt burden; and the ownership by the wealthy of the national debt.

The new Keynes Plan was designed to overcome these problems. Its centre-piece was a scheme for 'deferred earnings'. Excess private purchasing power would be mopped up by a heavily progressive surcharge on all incomes above an exempted minimum, made up of direct taxes and compulsory saving. The latter, credited to individual accounts in the Post Office Saving Bank, would be released in instalments after the war to counteract the expected post-war slump. As Professor Moggridge notes, 'the scheme had the advantage that it could operate through the existing arrangements for national insurance contributions'. Following criticisms of the original plan, Keynes proposed to 'provide for this deferred consumption without increasing the National Debt by a general capital levy after the war'; and to protect the poorest through family allowances – 5s or 25p a week per child – and an 'iron ration' of necessaries to be sold at low fixed prices. In estimating the size of the 'inflationary gap' – the amount by which civilian consumption would need to be reduced to enable output to be transferred to the war effort without prices rising –

Keynes, in the absence of official national income statistics, offered estimates, based on the work of Colin Clark, of national output and taxable income, the division of total spending between the government and private sector, and income distribution, all in 1939 prices. It then became relatively easy to calculate how much 'private outlay' had to be reduced to accommodate any desired increase in 'government outlay' at these prices, as well as the sacrifice required from each section of the community.

Keynes's plan had no influence on the budget of July 1940; he was better placed to continue his campaign of persuasion within the Treasury. Kingsley Wood's budget of April 1941 has been hailed as the first 'Keynesian' budget, not because it adopted the specific measures Keynes had proposed (though deferred pay survived in the form of a modest scheme for post-war tax credits), but because it was based, for the first time, on the national accounting framework developed, from Keynes's suggestions, by James Meade and others. Whether it marked general acceptance of the Keynesian Revolution is far more doubtful. The endorsement of the Keynes Plan by prominent anti-Keynesians like Hayek gives the clue to its popularity with economists and Treasury officials: it suggested a method of minimizing wartime inflation. As Jim Tomlinson has remarked: 'Keynesian arithmetic provided a theoretical rationale and quantification for policies which ran with rather than against the grain of the traditional Treasury stance on wartime finance.'

The debate sparked off by *How to Pay for the War* gave Keynes a chance to link his new economics to the political ideas of the Middle Way, ideas which he had espoused since the 1920s. 'Nature's way' (inflation) of first redistributing income from workers to entrepreneurs, and then taxing it, would no longer work, he said, because, in the new conditions of trade-union strength, rising prices would be matched by equivalent wage demands, which would either have to be conceded, defeating the object of reducing civilian consumption, or prohibited, bringing about industrial disruption. Stable prices were the quid pro quo for trade-union collaboration – a thought which goes back to his early days as a monetary reformer. The object of his plan was '*social*: to prevent the social evils of inflation now and later; to do this in a way which satisfies the popular sense of social justice; whilst maintaining adequate incentives to work and economy'. The significance of Keynes's proposals was thus twofold: they sought to circumvent the problem of 'cost push' inflation at full employment; and they claimed for the budget a role in social policy which went beyond macroeconomic stabilization.

In another respect, though, they went against the grain of left-wing thinking. For most socialists the war offered an opportunity for physical, rather than financial, planning. State allocation of manpower and supplies in accordance with 'national needs' would replace the 'chaos' of the market. Also, rationing of foodstuffs and clothing had a much more straightforward egalitarian appeal than 'forced saving'. The difference in principle was that Keynes's plan left the disposition of post-tax incomes to individual choice, while rationing required that individuals spent their money on things, and in the amounts, laid down by the state. 'I am seizing an opportunity', Keynes wrote to *The Times* on 18 April 1940 'to introduce a principle of policy which may come to be thought of as marking the line of division between the totalitarian and the free economy'. Similarly, the release of deferred pay, 'by allowing individuals to choose for themselves what they want, will save us from having to devise large-scale government plans of expenditure [after the war] which may not correspond so closely to personal need'. Keynes was once more staking a middle way between the '*invalidism* of the Left which has eaten up the wisdom and inner strength of many good causes' and the 'sclerotic' reaction of the Right to any tampering with the existing system. In practice, Keynes lost the argument to the central planners, and regulation of aggregate spending took second place to manpower planning, physical allocation of inputs, and rationing of consumer goods.

Keynes was far less involved with the famous 'Keynesian' White Paper on Employment Policy, published on 26 May 1944 (Cmd. 6527). Its first sentence – which Keynes thought 'is more valuable than the rest' – committed the government to the 'maintenance of a high and stable level of employment after the war'. But the text of the White Paper was a compromise between the Keynesians of the Economic Section of the Cabinet and the traditional sceptics of the Treasury, who felt that concessions had to be made to political pressures. Much of its analysis of the prospective unemployment problem was un-Keynesian, reflecting the view of Hubert Henderson that the problems of the British economy were on the supply rather than the demand side. Little thought was given about how to satisfy two of the conditions laid down in the White Paper for sustainable 'high employment': moderation in wage policy (the responsibility of employers and organized labour) and adequate labour mobility.

The international economy was the subject of the next Keynes Plan. The inherited gold standard/free-trade system had seemingly been damaged beyond repair by the First World War, the Great Depression, and the nationalist economics of the interwar years. The question was: could British full employment best be secured by a continuation of the Imperial Preference/Sterling Area arrangements built up in the 1930s, or did the war offer the chance of a 'single act of creation', impossible in peacetime, to restore a liberal system free of the deflationary bias which had wrecked the old one? This question engaged most of Keynes's attention and dwindling energy between 1941 and 1944. Its answer lay in the United States, because American policy would determine the shape of the post-war order.

Keynes's involvement with the United States provides an important context for understanding his economics. Those who take their Keynes solely from the 'closed economy' model of *The General Theory* forget that the problem which exercised him for most of his professional life arose from the effects of the unbalanced creditor position of the United States on the British economy. Most of his economic plans were concerned with ways of overcoming or offsetting this imbalance. They culminate in the establishment of the Bretton Woods system in 1944, and the negotiation of the American loan in 1945, as a result of which Britain tacitly accepted a junior role in an American-managed international economic order. But there was nothing inevitable about this culmination, and for much of his life Keynes actively explored alternatives.

In the 1920s, as we have seen, Keynes wanted to decouple the British (and, more generally, the European) financial system from that of the United States. But even in his *Tract* period he was not a currency floater. He wanted a 'managed' exchange-rate system – something consistent with stability of exchange rates for long periods. More often he hankered for a fixed exchange-rate system, with discretion and devices to give it flexibility. In both the early 1920s and the 1930s, when currencies floated against each other, he had proposed returning to a modified gold standard based at various times on wide bands, crawling pegs, automatic creditor adjustment, or supplementary reserve assets. He was convinced that any fixed exchange-rate system would break down if it was used as an instrument of deflation. Such a system worked best when supported by policies to maintain full employment over time. Stable exchange rates would, in turn, help keep the world growing in step and act as anti-inflationary discipline.

As Kingsley Martin records, Keynes's immediate response to the disintegration of the gold standard in 1931 was characteristic: 'At one stroke Britain has resumed the financial hegemony of the world,' he announced, 'chuckling like a boy who has just exploded a firework under some one he doesn't like.' The spontaneous emergence of a sterling bloc suggested to him a 'reputable sterling system for the Empire ... managed by the Bank of England and pivoted on London'. He applauded the Bank of England's nationalistic policy of sterilizing gold inflows to keep the pound undervalued against the dollar and franc, which remained on the gold standard – just as he had praised the same policy pursued by the Federal Reserve Board in the 1920s.

This euphoria did not last. Roosevelt's devaluation of the dollar in terms of gold on 19 April 1933 eliminated Britain's short-lived competitive advantage. Keynes now suggested that Britain and the United States might link their currencies together in a modified gold standard so long as they pursued reflationary policies in tandem. Nevertheless, on 4 July 1933 he proclaimed, 'President Roosevelt is Magnificently Right,' when Roosevelt scuppered the London World Economic Conference by denouncing all plans to stabilize currencies as 'the fetishes of so-called international bankers'. Keynes echoed: 'Let finance be primarily national.'

The way to make sense of these twists and turns is to remember that Keynes was offering advice he thought suited Britain best. The pound and dollar, he thought, might be safely linked provided certain conditions were met. He summed up his position in a letter to a German correspondent on 13 October 1936:

1) In general I remain in favour of independent national systems with fluctuating exchange rates.
2) Unless, however, a long period is considered, there need be no reason why the exchange rate should in practice be constantly fluctuating.
3) Since there are certain advantages in stability ... I am entirely in favour of practical measures towards de facto stability so long as there are no fundamental grounds for a different policy.
4) I would even go so far ... as to give some additional assurance as to the magnitude of the fluctuation which would be normally allowed ... Provided there was no actual pledge, I think that in most ordinary circumstances a margin of 10% should prove sufficient.

5) I would emphasise that the practicability of stability would depend (i) upon measures to control capital movements, and (ii) the existence of a tendency for broad wage movements to be similar in the different countries concerned.

Keynes's attitude to the United States softened in the 1930s. He visited it twice, in 1931 and 1934. On the second, and much more important visit, he went to study the New Deal, saw Roosevelt, and explained his new theory of effective demand in Washington and New York. Keynes was greatly impressed. 'Here, not in Moscow is the economic laboratory of the world,' he wrote to Felix Frankfurter on 30 May 1934. 'The young men who are running it are splendid. I am astonished at the competence, intelligence and wisdom. One meets a classical economist here and there who ought to have been thrown out of [the] window – but they mostly have been.' The commitment of the Administration, and of the younger section of the economics profession, to a policy of economic expansion was to be crucial in winning Keynes over to the idea that an American-led world economic system might not be as damaging to Britain's interests as he had feared.

There is a certain paradox, here, for Hitler's New Deal was much more coherent than Roosevelt's and much more successful in getting rid of unemployment. But except for a guarded reference to the advantages of totalitarianism in planning output as a whole, in the German preface to his *General Theory*, Keynes made no public comment on the Nazi economic system, either laudatory or critical. However, he freely condemned Nazism as a barbaric political system, and took to calling Germany and Italy 'brigand powers'. The main reason for Keynes's lack of approbation of Nazi economics was his detestation of the regime. But a subsidiary factor was that, unlike in the United States, there was no body of professional economists, in Germany or anywhere else in Europe outside Sweden, with whom he could seriously engage. The contribution of the Stockholm school apart, the technical discussion following the publication of Keynes's *General Theory of*

Employment, Interest and Money in 1936 was an Anglo-American affair. This is a neglected source of Keynes's simultaneous pull to America, and repulsion from Europe, which followed the breakdown of the supposedly self-regulating international economy in the 1930s.

On the other hand, although Hitler's Germany was in no sense a fit partner for Britain, Keynes at no time urged a preventive war to stop Germany. He approved of the Munich settlement, though not of Hitler's methods in extracting it, thought that whether Hitler seized Danzig or not did not matter in the least, and would have been content to let him take over the Ukraine if he could. As Professor Carr has shown, there were complicated reasons for all these attitudes, but avoidance of another Western European war, and giving Germany its outlet in the east, as part of the rebalancing of Europe he had advocated in 1919 and 1921, were the most important. The United States barely featured in his plans to contain the 'brigand powers'.

The United States was not at first involved in the European and Asian wars, and *all* the belligerents' plans for a post-war economic order left out the United States. Initially, these were based on the reasoning of the 1930s, when Britain, Germany, and Japan had tried to form economic blocs which discriminated against the United States, since none of them felt they could live with America's unbalanced competitive power. The United States, by contrast, had become increasingly internationalist, with Roosevelt's secretary of state, Cordell Hull, vociferous in support of free trade. Once involved in the war, its major war aim was to dismantle the neo-mercantilist blocs established by the other belligerents. (These hopes extended, more vaguely, to the even more autarkic system established by the USSR.) The defeat of Germany and Japan would automatically eliminate their systems; but the United States could also exert powerful pressure on its dependent ally, Britain.

The first post-war plan was produced by Germany. Dr Walther Funk, Hitler's Economics Minister, proclaimed a European 'New Order' in Paris on 25 July 1940. This called for a European economic bloc with fixed exchange rates and a central clearing union in Berlin. Relations with the United States would be on a barter basis. The purpose of the plan was to restore within Europe what Funk called 'an intelligent division of labour', while shielding Europe as a whole from the deflationary consequences of an international gold standard.

Keynes at the British Treasury saw much virtue in the Funk proposals. He wrote to Harold Nicolson on 20 November 1940: 'If Funk's plan is taken at its face value, it is excellent and just what we ourselves ought to be doing. If it is to be attacked, the way to do it would be to cast doubt and suspicion on its *bona fides*.' Even more striking was Keynes's formal response to the German plan on 1 December:

> It is not our purpose to reverse the roles proposed by Germany for herself and for her neighbours ... Germany must be expected and allowed to assume the measure of economic leadership which flows naturally from her own qualifications and her geographical position. Germany is the worst master the world has yet known. But, on terms of equality, she can be an efficient colleague.

On 25 April 1941, Keynes envisaged a sterling system including some European countries, free to discriminate against American goods if the United States 'persisted in maintaining an unbalanced creditor position'.

He received a rude jolt when he visited Washington from 7 May to 29 July 1941. As in 1915, Britain depended on purchases in neutral United States for which it could not pay. In December 1940, Roosevelt had announced 'Lend-Lease' – a scheme to provide Britain with supplies, not in exchange for borrowed money, as in the First World War, but for an undisclosed post-war 'consideration'. Keynes came as the emissary of a 'great & independent nation', inclined 'to ask as of right what they are only prepared to give us as a favour'. On 28 July, the day before he left, he was handed a State Department draft of the Lend-Lease agreement which, in Article VII, spelt out the 'consideration': a pledge by Britain to avoid 'discrimination against the importation' of American goods – in essence, a demand that Britain trade Imperial Preference for Lend-Lease. Keynes himself may have precipitated the American *démarche* by telling the State Department, on 25 June, that Britain might be forced to resort to discriminatory trade policies to balance her exports and imports after the war. When he saw Article VII, he exploded. His denunciations of 'Mr. Hull's lunatic proposals' went round Washington. All this seemed a rerun of the sour atmosphere of the First World War. But Keynes was now older, and wiser. Besides, in 1941 Britain had no realistic option but to meet American wishes, as, unlike in 1916, there was no hope of a negotiated peace. So Keynes retired to his country house, Tilton, in August to draft a new Keynes Plan. This was his famous proposal for a 'Clearing Union', which now included the United States, initialled on 8 September 1941.

The essential feature of the plan was that creditor countries would not be allowed to 'hoard' their surpluses, or charge punitive rates of interest for lending them out; rather they would be automatically available as cheap overdraft facilities to debtors through the mechanism of an international clearing bank whose depositors were the central banks of the union. However, he was still prepared to fall back on the alternative of a British-led currency bloc, maintained by 'Schachtian devices' if the United States refused to play. (Dr Schacht, Hitler's economics minister in the 1930s, had developed a successful system of bilateral trade agreements to balance Germany's external accounts.) A second draft, which Keynes initialled on 18 November 1941, added the 'highly substantive proposal' that membership of the Currency Union might be grouped by 'political and geographic units' such as the sterling area. These suggestions retain their interest as a possible model for a gradual return to a global fixed exchange-rate system today.

American requirements were spelt out explicitly once the United States entered the war in December 1941. The United States insisted that, in return for aid, Britain should pledge itself, after the war, to abandon trade discrimination. This pledge was incorporated into Article VII of the Lend-Lease Agreement signed on 23 February 1942, five days after the fall of Singapore to the Japanese. Keynes now realized that the economic bloc alternative was a non-starter. America would not finance the British war effort to allow Britain to emerge as head of a 'Schachtian' system which discriminated against American exports. Keynes had to apply himself to the intellectual problem of how to fit the British demand for freedom to pursue full employment policies into an American free-trade framework. He was forced to accept that the post-war world would be shaped by American power, as modified by American idealism and British brains. He would also have been less than Keynes, and less of an economist and liberal, had he not been seized by the possibility of using a unique historical moment to recreate an improved version of the liberal economic order which had collapsed in the First World War. Keynes also understood a moral and geopolitical fact. Assuming the defeat of Germany, the choice after the war would be between what he called 'the American and Russian bias' – that is, between world capitalism and autarkic socialism, with not much in between. 'Is there not much to be said', he wrote, 'for having a good try with the American bias first?'

Independently, the Americans had also been thinking about the post-war economic order. Harry Dexter White, a US Treasury official, produced a plan in March 1942. This was for a modified gold standard, to which was attached a modest adjustment facility in the shape of a Stabilization Fund on which subscribing members could draw up to the amount of subscriptions in their own currencies; a scheme which, by strictly limiting American liability, upheld, in effect, the orthodox doctrine of debtor adjustment. White's total adjustment facility (originally $5bn later $8bn) was much smaller than the total overdraft facility ($26bn) envisaged in the Keynes Plan; and strict conditions were attached to the drawing of quotas. Neither Keynes nor White saw each other's plans till the summer of 1942. Both were adopted as bargaining positions by their respective governments.

The Bretton Woods Agreement, signed on 22 July 1944, after two difficult negotiating sessions in Washington, reflected American rather than British views. British and American conflicts on such matters as exchange-rate management, access to reserves, tariff policy, and responsibility for adjustment reflected national interests, as filtered through the experiences of the interwar years and expectations of the future. Britain's negotiating achievements were limited to obtaining safeguards, postponements, and derogations within the framework of the American plan. The chief British success was to secure a 'scarce currency' clause which allowed debtor countries to discriminate against creditor countries under specified conditions.

According to James Meade and Lionel Robbins, members of the British negotiating teams who kept diaries, Keynes's performances at the two Washington conferences of September–October 1943 and July–August 1944 were mixtures of extraordinary eloquence, verbal as well as intellectual, and extraordinary rudeness to and about the Americans. After one negotiating session, Harry Dexter White told Robbins, 'Your Baron Keynes sure pees perfume.' Robbins wrote, after another, how 'The Americans sat entranced as the God-like visitor sang and the golden light played around'. On the other hand, Meade reported Carl Bernstein of the US Treasury 'smarting from Keynes's ill-manners'. (Keynes had said of one of his drafts: 'This is intolerable. It is yet another Talmud.') Keynes's bad manners as a negotiator no doubt reflected exhaustion and failing health, but also his frustration at Britain's impotence. This mingled sense of idealism and consciousness that America ultimately called the tune was true of all the British negotiators. 'In the world of the future we shall have to live more by our wits,' noted Lionel Robbins. The trouble was that wits, too, had to be muted, in deference to the American fear of being made suckers 'especially by the diabolically clever Lord Keynes'.

In the House of Lords on 23 May 1944, Keynes commended the agreed Anglo-American plan in terms both of idealism and necessity. 'What alternative is open to us ... ?' Unlike in the First World War, he now took pride in the fact that 'in thus waging the war without counting the ultimate cost we – and we alone of the United Nations – have burdened ourselves with a weight of deferred indebtedness to other countries beneath which we shall stagger'. Specifically, without the new framework afforded by the Anglo-American agreement,

> London must necessarily lose its international position, and the arrangements ... of the sterling area would fall to pieces. To suppose that a system of bilateral and barter agreements, with no one who owns sterling knowing just what he can do with it ... is the best way of encouraging the Dominions to centre their financial systems on London, seems to me pretty near frenzy.

The 'technique of little Englandism' was incompatible with England's imperial heritage. 'With our own resources so greatly impaired and encumbered, it is only if sterling is firmly placed in an international setting that the necessary confidence in it can be sustained.' To place American power and money, on terms, behind Britain's 'impaired and encumbered' system of earning its living was thus the ultimate object of the 'special relationship' which the war had made necessary.

The defeat of Keynes's Clearing Union plan had highlighted the problem of financing Britain's prospective current account deficit after the war. Keynes eventually estimated this at between $6bn and \$7bn over a three-year 'transitional' period. On 17 August 1945, three days after the Japanese surrender, the United States abruptly cancelled Lend-Lease. From now on Britain would have to pay for all supplies, including those already ordered. The Clearing Union proposal had been explicitly designed to make balance of payments assistance from America after the war unnecessary. 'Overdrafts' from the clearing bank would have been automatically available to plug Britain's post-war 'dollar gap'. Britain's quota from the IMF was far too small for this, and, in any event, only a country with a convertible currency could exercise its 'drawing rights'. Sterling devaluation was ruled out, partly because Britain's import surplus was too large, partly because 'repudiation' of Britain's sterling debts (totalling \$14bn) would have killed off the sterling area. Isolationists of Right and Left favoured strict trade controls, but, Keynes asked Beaverbrook on 27 April 1945:

> Do you really favour a barter system of trade which would mean, in practice, something very near a state monopoly of imports and exports à la Russe? Do you welcome an indefinite continuance of strict controls and (probably) severer rationing? Do you look forward to our stepping down, for the time being, to the position of a second-class power...?

So American help was all that was left.

Keynes hoped that assistance from the United States would take the form of a grant, or at least an interest-free loan. Hugh Dalton, Labour's chancellor of the exchequer, recorded that 'Keynes in his talks with Ministers just before leaving for Washington, was almost starry-eyed. He was very confident that...he could get six billion dollars as a free gift...Nor did he...say much to us about the "strings".' The banker Robert Brand said: 'When I listen to Lord Keynes talking, I seem to hear those coins jingling in my pocket.' Soon after Keynes arrived in Washington on 5 September as joint head of the British delegation, he realized the mood had changed. Over incredibly sticky negotiations which lasted three months the six billion dollar 'free gift' was whittled down to a loan of $3.75bn at 2% interest, with the 'string' that sterling be made convertible a year after the agreement was ratified. This forfeited Britain's transitional protection under the Bretton Woods Agreement. Having been over-optimistic at the start, Keynes drove a bewildered and angry Labour government, step by step, to accept progressively less favourable terms. His health and temper collapsed. In the end, he was replaced as joint head of the British delegation by Sir Edward Bridges, who agreed the final settlement.

Keynes's eloquent defence of his handiwork in the House of Lords on 18 December, twelve days after the loan agreement was signed, put the negotiations in the context of events as they had unfolded since the First World War. There was first the argument from necessity. The alternative to the loan agreement, he said, 'is to build up a separate economic bloc which excludes Canada and consists of countries to which we already owe more than we can pay, on the basis of their agreeing to lend us money they have not got and buy only from us and one another goods we are unable to supply'. Secondly, there was the appeal of a shared, reconstituted liberalism:

> The separate economic blocs and all the friction and loss of friendship they must bring with them are expedients to which one may be driven in a hostile world . . . But it is surely crazy to prefer that. Above all, this determination to make trade truly international and to avoid the establishment of economic blocs which limit and restrict commercial intercourse outside them, is plainly an essential condition of the world's best hope, an Anglo-American understanding . . . Some of us, in the tasks of war and more lately in those of peace, have learnt by experience that our two countries can work together. Yet it would be only too easy for us to walk apart. I beg those who look askance at these plans to ponder deeply and responsibly where it is they think they want to go.

The familiar context of Keynesian economics is the Great Depression of the 1930s – the collapse of the world economy. But a more persistent context was the unbalanced creditor position of the United States. For the first ten years after the First World War, the United States boomed, while Britain slumped. Keynes saw British unemployment as a problem of sterling's overvaluation against the dollar. From this point of view, his *General Theory* is an addendum to, rather than the culmination of, his line of thought – the theory of a deep world slump when no amount of monetary manipulation can restore full employment.

Following the collapse of the gold standard in 1931, the world economy broke up into trading blocs based on 'key' currencies. It was as manager of an imperial payments system known as the Sterling Area that Britain went to war with Germany in 1939.

It took the Second World War to put paid to Keynes's hope of a British-controlled payments system as the monetary framework for the British economy. Much shared idealism and responsibility went into the making of the Bretton Woods system. Nevertheless it was the end of British monetary independence. The sterling system could not survive unless it was bolstered by the dollar. Keynes's lifetime spans the passage from control to dependence.

Chapter 6
Keynes's legacy

Any assessment of the work of a past master is bound to reflect the state of mind of its time. At present (July 1995), Keynes's reputation is precariously poised. Ten years ago, one might have said that the Keynesian era was dead and buried. Nigel Lawson, then Britain's chancellor of the exchequer, did say so. 'The conquest of inflation', he declared in his Mais Lecture of 1984, 'should . . . be the objective of macroeconomic policy. And . . . the creation of conditions conducive to growth and employment . . . should be . . . the objective of microeconomic policy.' There was no commitment to full employment. Rather, the idea was to free up markets as much as possible and accept whatever level of activity they produced. Today, there is some reaction back to Keynes, partly because the deflationary policies pursued over the last fifteen years have left high and persisting unemployment in their wake – as, indeed, Keynes predicted such policies would. Unemployment in the European Union has been rising since the 1970s, stands at 10% of the work-force today and has not fallen by much during the recovery from the recession of 1991–2. It is as if the combined population of Denmark, Ireland, and Switzerland was producing nothing at all – hardly a triumph for market forces.

Although monetarism failed to deliver stable prices and tolerable employment, Keynesian policy as we knew it is not restored. Most governments believe that Keynesian remedies for unemployment will be either ineffective or mischievous, much as they did when Keynes first started advocating them. This partly reflects the view that most unemployment today is 'structural' not Keynesian; that is, it reflects not a shortage of demand but the wrong structure of capital and relative wages. Furthermore, it is widely believed that structural maladjustment came about (or was allowed to continue for as long as it did) as a consequence of the 'Keynesian' policy of creating or maintaining employment in unproductive or loss-making occupations. Even if some part, at least, of current unemployment is conceded to have its origins in a deficiency of aggregate demand, it is believed that expanding demand would cancel the gains on the inflation front, achieved at such cost, since 1979.

In short, Keynesian policies come to us today wrapped up in a history of rising inflation, unsound public finance, expanding statism, collapsing corporatism, and general ungovernability, all of which have seemed inseparable from the Keynesian cure for the afflictions of industrial society. We do not want to traverse that path again. By the 1980s, Keynes, who was praised for having saved the world from Marxism, had joined Marx as the God that failed.

The question of how the Keynesian age came to generate expectations which undermined the Keynesian revolution calls for both a theoretical and a historical explanation. Perhaps a historian is as well placed as anybody to offer one. Both sides of the explanation will be personal to the writer, since there is little agreement on 'what went wrong'. But anyone who wants to keep the spirit of Keynes alive has to face the failures of Keynesianism honestly, without always trying to shield the Master from the mistakes of the disciples. In essence, the Keynesian revolution was ruined by over-ambition – *hubris* might be a better word – driven by impatience and backed by unwarranted claims to both theoretical and practical knowledge. The monetarist counter-revolution was a plea for more modesty, and greater trust in the spontaneous forces of the market.

It is hard to fit Keynes himself into the Keynesian versus Monetarist debate, because his *General Theory* was built to understand the world of the 1930s, not the world of the 1960s or 1970s. It is perfectly possible to get (qualified) monetarist conclusions out of *The General Theory* on certain assumptions about expectations, but these were not the purposes for which the book was written. To understand much of what Keynes had to say about money and credit and exchange rates, the banking system and financial markets, the reader needs to turn to the *Tract on Monetary Reform* and the *Treatise on Money*. For those who seek contemporary inspiration in Keynes, three other facts are worth remembering. First, although he was intellectually over-confident – a trait inherited by his followers – he was notably modest about what policy could achieve in a free society – something which his followers tended to ignore. Secondly, his social aims were, as he put it, 'moderately conservative'. There is nothing in Keynes's social philosophy, or the Liberalism of his day, which would have supported the seemingly relentless expansion of the welfare activities of the state which contributed so heavily to the fiscal crises of the 1970s. Finally, he was an apostle of growth not for its own sake, but only as a means to leisure and civilized living. In fact, he argued in the late 1920s that 'technological' unemployment was a sign that the economic problem was being solved. 'The full employment policy by means of investment is only one particular application of an intellectual theorem,' he wrote to T. S. Eliot in 1945. 'You can produce the result just as well by consuming more or working less ... Less work is the ultimate solution [to the unemployment] problem.'

For twenty-five years after Keynes's death, his revolution prospered. Most economists accepted 'the new economics' (even Milton Friedman said in 1966, 'We are all Keynesians now,' a phrase repeated by Richard Nixon in 1972); most governments committed themselves to maintain full employment. To be sure, not all who called themselves 'Keynesians' accepted *The General Theory* as gospel. Indeed, there was a retreat from Keynes's own theory. As a result of Patinkin's work (1956), classical theory was partly rehabilitated, in that the downward rigidity of money-wages was seen as the *essential* obstacle to full employment, as Arthur Pigou had always claimed. In Leijonhufvud's reinterpretation (1968), Keynes's 'unemployment equilibrium' was to be understood as a rhetorical device; his was a disequilibrium theory emphasizing co-ordination failures – an approach which stressed the continuity of *The General Theory* with the *Treatise on Money*, thus narrowing its distance from the monetary disequilibrium theorists of the 1930s. However, a world with downwardly rigid money-wages and the ever-present possibility of a collapse in private investment is still a world which leaves a necessary role for government *policy* to maintain continuous full employment.

Apart from this, three aspects of Keynes's legacy seemed secure. First, practically all economists accepted Keynes's macroeconomic framework. Keynes had invented a new branch of economics, macroeconomics, the study of the behaviour of the economic system as a whole, rather than the study of the behaviour of individuals, firms, or industries. 'Students in the 1960s were taught that we could model the economy, diagnose the state of effective demand and devise appropriate fiscal interventions.' Secondly, *The General Theory* had provided the conceptual breakthrough for constructing national accounts. The consequent mushrooming of economic statistics was hugely influential in the development of econometrics, which, in turn (it might then have been said), provided a secure forecasting basis for macroeconomic policy. Finally, Keynes had restored faith in the capitalist system. Keynesian economics had helped write Fascism, Communism, and some kinds of socialism out of the history of the developed world.

Keynesian theory had also contributed to the emergence of development economics – the study of economic growth in poor countries. Roy Harrod, in particular, extended the Keynesian explanation of short-run unemployment into a model of self-sustaining growth, emphasizing the central role of physical investment. The mid-1960s saw an upsurge of faith in the power of macroeconomic policy to deliver not just full employment, but high rates of growth, and many other desirable social objectives.

Ten years later the counter-revolution against Keynes was in full swing. Milton Friedman's restatement of the quantity theory of money in 1956 was followed, in 1968, by the most influential macroeconomic paper of the post-war years. In this, Friedman claimed that attempts by governments to reduce unemployment below the 'natural rate' set by market institutions led only to accelerating inflation. In 1976, the Keynesian revolution in policy was officially declared dead in its birthplace, when Britain's Labour prime minister, James Callaghan, announced that the option of 'spending our way out of recession no longer existed' and in the past had worked only by 'injecting bigger and bigger doses of inflation into the economy'. Throughout the world, price stability rather than full employment became the stated goal of macroeconomic policy.

The monetarist counter-revolution called into question the most fundamental aspects of Keynes's legacy. If nominal changes (changes in money) affect prices, not output, in the long run, as Friedman claimed, we do not need macroeconomics, only an updated quantity theory of money. If, as Friedman claimed, the economy is 'inherently more cyclically stable' than Keynes supposed, while macroeconomic interventions are subject to 'long and variable lags', not only do we not need counter-cyclical policy, it will be destabilizing. If we do not need counter-cyclical policy, we do not need large macroeconomic forecasting models. Finally, Keynesian macroeconomic policy did not preserve capitalism from socialism, but led towards it by the need for increasing political intervention in the microeconomy to make macroeconomic policy work. Instead of trying to stimulate the economy through mixtures of public spending and planning, governments should concentrate on controlling inflation and improving the working of the market system.

Rightly or wrongly, the fate of the Keynesian revolution has been determined by events. The depression of the 1930s gave rise to it; the 1950s and 1960s seemed to vindicate it; the 'slumpflation' of the 1970s (the combination of high unemployment and high inflation) ended it. The legacy of the 1980s is ambiguous, and should betoken a modest revival.

The 1950s and most of the 1960s were a capitalist golden age. By historical standards, unemployment was exceptionally low, growth in real incomes exceptionally fast, economies exceptionally stable; all achieved at a very modest cost in inflation. These successes were widely attributed to Keynesian policies, inspired by Keynesian theory.

Then prosperity started to unravel. From the late 1960s inflation *and* unemployment began to edge up, growth to slow down. In the OECD countries, consumer prices, which had risen by 3.1% a year on average in 1960–8, rose by 10.5% a year in 1973–9. Unemployment, 3.1% a year on average in the first period, was 5.1% in the second. The growth of real GDP per capita slowed down from 3.9% in 1960–8 to 1.9% in 1973–9. In 1971, growing macroeconomic (including external payments) imbalances brought down the system of fixed, but adjustable, exchange rates established at Bretton Woods in 1944, even before the first oil-price shock of 1973–4.

Having been credited with success, Keynesian policy was blamed for subsequent failure. Both conclusions are questionable. Did economic ideas, Keynesian or otherwise, have much influence on what governments did? Did the policies of governments make much difference to what happened? The answer to both questions is almost certainly yes, but the interactions between the three realms of ideas, policies, and events are so complicated that no account of their relationship is likely to command general assent. We can at least try to distinguish between the rhetorical and technical uses of economic ideas, and avoid calling Keynesian the general expansion of state activity after the war, and attributing to Keynesian policy all the consequences, good and bad, which followed from this expansion. As Christopher Allsopp has written, 'The development of Welfare States, industrial intervention, and public expenditure programmes . . . has little to do with . . . the economics of Keynes . . . It is necessary . . . not to lose sight of the fundamental point that the original message was minimalist in spirit.' Beyond this, it is rhetorically useful to be reminded that Keynes was against inflation, nationalization, planning, equalization of incomes, etc., if only because many who have advocated these things have done so in his name.

In trying to assess the influence of Keynesian policy on post-war events, an initial problem is to understand what is meant by Keynesian policy. In France and Italy, for example, what would now be called active supply-side policies were routinely mislabelled 'Keynesian'. A more relevant test is the commitment to maintain full employment. But only in Britain and the United States was such a commitment given, and even then ambiguously. The British Employment White Paper of 1944 pledged the government to maintain a 'high and stable' level of employment. What was high? What was stable?

Jim Tomlinson has suggested a more stringent test. The Keynesian revolution, he says, 'should be defined in terms of an attempt to legitimize (budget) deficits as a device for use when the level of aggregate demand required stimulation'. Keynesian policy may then be said to be in operation when budget deficits are deliberately incurred to raise the level of output. On this test, there was no Keynesian policy during the height of the 'golden age' because, as R. C. O. Matthews pointed out in 1968, 'the [British] Government, so far from injecting demand into the system, has persistently had a large current account surplus'. The same was true for the United States until 1964. Similarly, there was no active demand management policy in the most successful 'golden age' economies, Germany and Japan. The implication is that the post-war world did not need, and did not get, a Keynesian revolution in policy.

In *The General Theory*, Keynes had talked of a happy 19th-century 'conjuncture' which allowed employment to be reasonably full without government intervention. It may be that the 'golden age' should be seen as resulting from a similar conjuncture. As Crafts and Woodward point out, across the developed world there were 'widespread opportunities to imitate American technology, to contract low productivity agriculture, and to exploit cheap energy'. The opportunities for technological catch-up gave capital a high marginal productivity, leading to high private investment demand. A high rate of productivity growth allowed a sufficient rise in real incomes to satisfy workers' aspirations while keeping unit costs fairly stable. Governments also consumed a much higher proportion of the national income than they had before the war. As John Hicks put it in 1977: 'The combination of more rapid technical progress (surely a fact) with the socialist tendencies which increased demand for collective goods (surely also a fact) could have produced such a boom without the added stimulus of Keynesian policies.'

In this happy conjuncture a key role was played by the United States. In practice, only the United States enjoyed the luxury of an 'autonomous' macroeconomic policy. Under the gold-exchange-rate system established at Bretton Woods only the United States was on the gold standard; other countries held most of their reserves in dollars. Monetary conditions for the system as a whole were set by American financial policy, with other countries' macroeconomic policy being limited to maintaining their currencies' chosen exchange rate with the dollar. Under Truman and Eisenhower, American budgetary policy was conservative, interest rates were low, the balance of trade in surplus. Till the mid-1960s, the United States provided most countries with a reasonably secure anti-inflationary anchor, while supplying them with enough liquidity to prevent the deflationary contractions associated with a pure gold standard. The stability of the monetary regime allowed a progressive liberalization of the payments and trading system which, as Adam Smith would have predicted, was highly favourable to the growth of real incomes. Finally, there were *ad hoc* injections of demand from the United States – notably through Marshall Aid and the Korean war – which had the same stimulating effects as the Californian gold discoveries and the 'small wars' of the mid-19th century. In short, it was the Pax Americana which secured a rough and ready macroeconomic balance across the 'free world' during the golden age, much as the Pax Britannica had done in the 19th century. The existence of a buoyant international economy (unlike in the 1930s) made national economic problems much more tractable.

However, if purposeful Keynesian policy cannot explain the golden age, the explicit or implicit commitment to avoid a collapse in demand – and just as important, the belief that Keynesian policy would work if required – may well have secured the expectations ('state of confidence') necessary to sustain the private investment boom for so long. In particular, in the 1950s Keynesianism seemed to have erected a decisive barrier to the advance of socialism, whether in the form of public ownership or national planning. The subsequent identification of Keynesianism with a disproportionate growth of the public sector accompanied by growing labour militancy was crucial in destroying the psychological or *expectational* function of the Keynesian revolution – the belief that it would make the world safe for capitalism and capitalists.

It is worth pursuing the 19th-century parallel a little further. The boom of the 1850s and 1860s was followed by the depression of the 1870s through to the 1890s, which, as has often been pointed out, was not a slump in the 1930s sense, but a mixed period of prosperity and depression, with enormous technological restructuring accompanied by a shift of competitive dynamism from Britain to Germany and the United States. This is not totally dissimilar to what happened from the 1970s onwards, with competitive advantage shifting this time to the Pacific rim. What was missing from the earlier period was the phenomenon of 'stagflation'. There was heavy unemployment for much of the 1880s, but prices fell. In contrast, was the boom of the 1950s and 1960s 'artificially' prolonged by Keynesian policy?

According to the standard Keynesian story, the long boom was ended by the oil-price shock of 1973-4, though it was acknowledged that the path to this débâcle was strewn with policy mistakes and unexplained 'sociological' happenings like the wages explosion in 1968. But the deterioration of macroeconomic performance had been evident from at least the mid-1960s. It coincided with the switch to active Keynesian policies.

In the 1960s, Keynesianism was universalized, 'came into its own', in a double sense: the use of fiscal policy to balance economies was extended to France, Italy, Germany, and to a lesser extent Japan; and fiscal policy became more active and ambitious as fears of recession revived. Broadly speaking, while early Keynesian interest concentrated on securing the full use of existing resources, the Keynesianism of the 1960s tried to secure the full use of potential resources – i.e. growth in the productive capacity of the economy with the object of restraining cost-push inflation and meet the increasing 'social demands' being placed on the economy. What David Marquand (1988) has called the social democratic phase of Keynesianism is associated with a move to the Left in politics, and the serious use, for the first time, of budgetary policy to shift demand from the private to the public sector. The budget simultaneously became the agent of demand management, growth, and welfare. From the 1960s the share of public spending in GDP everywhere started to rise. The most significant macroeconomic episode, from the global point of view, was the Kennedy–Johnson tax cut and 'great society' spending programmes of 1964–6. In retrospect, though it was not evident at the time, this, together with the inflationary financing of the Vietnam War, ended the United States' role as the world's anti-inflationary anchor.

We can identify several plausible reasons for the shift from full employment to growth. In the United States, the observed tendency for unemployment to be a little higher at the peak of each cycle in the 1950s (though the average for the 1950s, at just over 5%, was close enough to the target rate of 4%) revived the old Keynesian fear of the 'secular stagnation' of mature economies. It suggested a growing output gap – the gap between the actual annual rate growth of output and its potential growth rate. Rejecting the idea that higher unemployment might be caused by technological factors like automation, the president's Council of Economic Advisers suggested that demand expansion could lower unemployment to 4% without 'unacceptable' price inflation, James Tobin arguing that the evils of 'small increases in prices' had been 'greatly exaggerated'. The Keynesian promise that demand expansion could achieve faster growth fed the politicians' desire to boost the American growth rate to avoid losing the ideological war (as well as the arms race) against the Soviet Union, which in the 1950s was trumpeting prodigious growth rates and dramatic technological achievements like Sputnik.

In Europe, resort to deficit finance stemmed from a fear that labour shortages would slow down growth (the erection of the Berlin Wall in 1961 stemmed the flow of cheap labour from East to West Germany); from the fear that the opening-up of domestic economies to free trade and capital flows, both globally and as a result of the formation of the European Economic Community in 1958, would make them more vulnerable to external shocks; and from the re-equipment of left-wing parties, long out of power, with up-to-date (that is, non-Marxist) ideologies. Keynesian growth policy seemed to be what was left when plentiful supply, protectionism, and obsolete ideologies were removed from the picture. In slow-growing Britain, growth policy was adopted to enable it to 'catch up' with industrial rivals like Germany and France. Japan resorted to deficit financing in 1965 when it started to lose key post-war instruments like tariffs and control over capital movements. Common to all countries was the belief that fast or faster growth was needed to raise the feasible real wage, and win trade-union support for wage restraint by making possible the expansion of welfare programmes.

In the 1960s, developing countries, some recently decolonized, embarked on state-led industrialization designed to enable them to catch up with rich ones. Growth would be accelerated by redirecting underemployed rural labour to heavy industry. The Keynesian-trained Argentinian economist Raoul Prebisch developed a 'terms of trade' argument for public investment in import-substituting manufactures. The result was a series of public investment booms within a framework of state ownership and indicative planning, largely financed by foreign borrowing.

Expectation that the rate of capital accumulation would fall was not unreasonable after post-war reconstruction and 'catch-up' had run their course. Much more questionable was the extension of Keynesian thinking from the short-run problem of securing full employment of existing resources to the problem of increasing the growth of these resources. For 'growth' Keynesians, active demand management (including fiscal deficits) was required not just to prevent or offset recessions but to realize the economy's long-run growth *potential*, an altogether more elusive idea. Keynes himself would have said – in fact he did say – that at full employment any exogenous injection of demand leads to inflation. This is the 'special case' to which classical economics applied, when faster growth of output can come about only through increased productivity and improved technique – matters on which Keynes had nothing distinctive to say. The growth Keynesians argued, *au contraire*, that productivity growth was endogenous to the growth process. The rate of output growth depended on the rate of growth of investment; the faster investment could be induced to grow, the larger would be the productivity gains, owing to the effect of dynamic economies of scale, leading to a 'virtuous circle' of rising productivity, greater competitiveness, and higher growth. Given sufficient total demand, output could always be induced to rise more than proportionately to the input of labour. Thus high employment was no barrier to demand-led expansion: growth, in the jargon, was demand, not supply constrained.

Demand expansion went hand in hand with indicative planning. In the British National Plan of 1965, indicated growth rates were worked out for each sector over a five-year period to raise the expectations of businessmen. But the key indicator was the projected growth of public spending. This would tell industrial sectors how much they needed to expand capacity, and at the same time guarantee that the increased output would be bought. Thus public spending emerged as the real engine of growth – a fateful conjuncture in Keynesian political economy. Governments also encouraged company mergers to realize minimum efficient scale. Devaluation was added as an instrument to help lift economies onto higher growth paths, rather than simply to overcome disequilibria in the balance of payments as envisaged at Bretton Woods.

In retrospect, all the presuppositions underpinning the dash for growth, in developed and developing countries alike, turned out to be intellectually and politically insecure. No one in fact knew how to make an economy grow faster over time than it was actually growing. Did the causation run from productivity growth to output growth or from output growth to productivity growth? Economists disagreed. Again, the Keynesians were remarkably sanguine about the effects of the growth of the public sector on productivity growth, wage behaviour, and business expectations. They thought that a little inflation (how much?) was stimulating, and had no inkling of inflationary expectations. Finally, they greatly exaggerated the extent of 'disguised' rural unemployment in developing countries, and hence the benefits to growth to be obtained by transferring these supposedly costless resources into industrial production. If there is a common theme linking these presuppositions, it was that the state is wise and the market is stupid.

Even Keynesians would now concede that the economic and social goals of the 1960s were over-ambitious. The record is clear: by the decade's end the OECD inflation rate had doubled from 3% to 6%, without any improvement in real variables. The rising inflation which was the real legacy of the growth Keynesianism of the 1960s set Keynesian macroeconomic policy an impossible task in the 1970s. Once inflation had been let loose, government interventions were bound to be seriously destabilizing, involving either acceptance of higher unemployment to check the rise in prices, or acceptance of higher inflation to check the rise in unemployment. The oscillation of policy between these choices produced a rising 'misery index' (inflation plus unemployment) for most of the 1970s. Monetarism gained respectability by being able to explain worsening stagflation in terms of the interaction between 'stop-go' Keynesian macroeconomic policy, and wage behaviour which adapted ever more quickly to inflationary expectations.

In the most general sense, excessive pressure of demand led to what a classical economist would have predicted: a worldwide explosion in costs due to supply shortages. The wages explosion in the West, starting in 1968, had its counterpart in the rise in raw material and energy prices, starting in 1972 and culminating in the fourfold increase in oil prices in 1973–4, which reduced the real wage warranted at full employment for industrial countries. Direct controls over wages ('incomes policies') broke down as the decade progressed, producing a squeeze on profits, which could be offset only by pumping more money into the public sector. Western countries became, in the phrase of the day, 'ungovernable'.

Eventually governments had had enough. In face of the second oil price rise of 1979–80, Western governments tightened fiscal and monetary policy, bringing about the most severe slump since the 1930s. Developing countries, which had maintained their public investment booms throughout the 1970s by borrowing recycled petrodollars at negative real interest rates, found themselves faced with crippling foreign debt burdens as export earnings collapsed, real interest rates rose to punitive levels, and foreign investment dried up. In return for rescheduling and new loans, the IMF imposed tough stabilization packages. World-wide, state-led growth policies had precisely the opposite effect to those intended: they had raised, not lowered, the cost of producing goods and services, and they had lowered, not raised, the capacity of economies to produce marketable output. The Keynesian age was over.

Even at this distance, it is hard to disentangle the specific Keynesian responsibility for these disasters from the more general climate of opinion and economic and social pressures causing governments and economies to behave in the way they did. The overestimate of the power of macroeconomic instruments was certainly important; but just as significant was a fatalistic acceptance, by both Left and Right, of a collectivist and corporatist future, made inevitable, so it seemed, by the increasing scale of business organization, the growth of encompassing pressure groups, and the demand for an increasing range of social and economic entitlements. After 1974–5, when governments had truly lost power to 'manage' their economies, the worst that can be said about Keynesianism was that it presented a barrier to new ideas and the development of alternative political strategies. For by this point in time the Keynesian revolution could not renew itself. It had spawned pathologies inhospitable to its remedies, and it had no intellectual or political resources left to understand them, or deal with them. Keynes cannot be blamed for this exhaustion. Nevertheless, certain aspects of his legacy proved troubling, in so far as they appeared to paralyse criticism from within the

Keynesian camp of extensions and applications of his theory to problems and situations for which it was not intended.

First, two incautious phrases in *The General Theory* gave a rhetorical warrant for the belief that public spending is better than private spending. Keynes conceived that the maintenance of full employment might require a 'somewhat comprehensive socialisation of investment'; he also said that if the Treasury paid people to dig holes and fill them up unemployment would fall 'and the real income of the community, and its capital wealth also, would probably become a good deal greater than it actually is'. However, Keynes was always alert to the effect of policy on business psychology. He understood that excessive state spending would undermine confidence in the direction of policy and raise funding problems for the government, which would jeopardize the aim of maintaining a low long-term real rate of interest. No one has more eloquently or succinctly summarized the mechanism of the 'inflation tax' than Keynes in 1923: 'A government can live by this means when it can live by no other. It is the form of taxation which the public finds hardest to evade and even the weakest government can enforce, when it can enforce nothing else.' He understood that if public finance is judged unsound it will not be able to fulfil its genuine Keynesian purpose, as forward-looking agents take steps to protect themselves from the risk of repudiation or monetization of government debt. Yet he never explicitly discussed how much of the community's spending could be safely or efficiently left to the state in a free society.

Secondly, there was no clear guidance in *The General Theory* as to what Keynes meant by full employment, either conceptually or statistically. A 'general theory' of employment which nourishes the belief that the level of employment is entirely determined in the goods market, and not at all in the labour market, is seriously misnamed. To be sure, in one passage Keynes distinguished between voluntary and involuntary unemployment, or as it was later put between 'classical' and 'Keynesian' unemployment, but his rhetorical purpose was to deny classical explanations of unemployment, and these were also ignored by his followers. Richard Kahn has testified to the fact that 'the concept of "voluntary unemployment" left me very cold' and that the distinction between the two types of unemployment 'has not proved to have any practical significance'. The reason is that *The General Theory* can be read as saying that if the state controls the wages fund and allocates labour, voluntary unemployment can always be converted into involuntary employment, and the rate of unemployment reduced to zero – as indeed it was in the Soviet Union. Keynes did not think like this, but his more collectivist followers, influenced by wartime planning, did, and there is nothing in *The General Theory* which explicitly says that voluntary unemployment is a choice which, in a free society, can or should be dealt with only by changing labour market incentives.

One has to go outside *The General Theory* to discover what Keynes habitually thought about the nature of unemployment. In *The General Theory*, he adapted, and clothed in new terms, a much older distinction between 'normal' unemployment, related to slowly changing labour market institutions, and 'abnormal' unemployment resulting from a cyclical downturn. He thought that the order of magnitude of 'normal' unemployment in Britain was about 5% – the pre-1914 average, leaving 5% in the 1920s, and nearer 10% in the 1930s, 'abnormal'. Thus as late as 16 December 1944, he wrote to Beveridge, 'No harm in aiming at 3 per cent unemployment, but I shall be surprised if we succeed.' Keynes also seems to have thought of 'normal' unemployment as that level of unemployment at which money-wages (and prices) are stable. When unemployment is above normal, money-wages fall, when it is below normal, they rise. This is close to the neo-Keynesian idea of the Non-Accelerating Inflation Rate of Unemployment (NAIRU) – the level of unemployment required to contain inflation. But it was left to non-Keynesians to draw the conclusion that the only feasible way of lowering the level of 'normal' unemployment (or the NAIRU) in a free society was through labour-market reforms. The Keynesian obsession with incomes policies left the defence of contractual freedom to the monetarists.

Thirdly, Keynes bequeathed no adequate theory of prices. Keynes himself cannot be accused of being soft on inflation. Not only had he graphically analysed the rotting effect of inflation on the social system of capitalism, but in 1920, with British consumer prices rising by 20% a year (the same as in 1975), he had urged a severe dose of 'dear money' and savage public expenditure cuts as the only alternative to state socialism: 'I would do this because I put very high the danger of going on with our present diseases without a drastic and unpleasant cure. And I would do it though I knew I risked a depression and possibly a crisis.' And he wrote in 1940: 'With all unorthodox [i.e. socialist] methods of control ... excluded, I feel myself that I should give today exactly the same advice that I gave then.' Delay in imposing and sticking to a 'dear money' policy in the mid-1970s made the subsequent situation much worse than it need have been.

This point can be generalized. In the pre-Keynesian era, the price level fell in a depression, rose in a boom, and on average stayed the same. It was thus easy for Keynes to be both an expansionist *and* a price stabilizer: in fact it could be shown that stability of the price level *required* that spending be increased when prices were falling. In the Keynesian era, prices went on rising during both upturn and downturn, though at different rates. The achievement of Keynesian policy in the 1970s was to change the popular perception that unemployment was an unacceptable cost of *laissez-faire* into the perception that it was an acceptable price for reducing inflation. Nor was this just ideological prejudice. Keynesian policy to expand employment is *unusable* until inflationary expectations have disappeared from the system, since if inflation is expected to rise workers will simply demand higher wages.

How did this perverse situation come about? Despite Keynes's own anti-inflationary credentials, the models derived from *The General Theory* were constant price models: they focused, that is, on inadequate, not excess demand. But a 'general theory' of money must include both possibilities and intermediate positions, and it is quite true that *The General Theory* accepted the quantity theory of money as valid at full employment: 'So long as there is unemployment, *employment* will change in the same proportion as the quantity of money; and when there is full employment, *prices* will change in the same proportion as the quantity of money.' More realistically, Keynes acknowledged that inflation could start before full employment was reached – he referred to 'positions of semi-inflation' when output still rises but prices rise more – owing to structural rigidities (skills and geographical mismatches) and trade unions' ability, as the labour market tightened, to push up wages ahead of productivity. In such a situation, is aggregate demand still to be considered deficient? Keynes did not say. Should demand management aim to maintain what Abba Lerner called 'low full employment' and price stability, or 'high full employment' with controls on wages and prices? Keynes did not say. He confined himself to the observation that the task of restraining wage push was 'a political rather than an economic problem'; he was 'inclined to turn a blind eye to the wages problem in a full employment economy'.

In place of a theory of inflation, there was an empirical observation dating from 1958, the Phillips Curve, showing a stable relationship over time between the level of unemployment and the rate of change of money-wages and, by later inference, prices. Keynes's grey area of 'semi-inflation' became the 'safe zone' of the Phillips Curve, within which governments were said to have a 'menu of choice' between degrees of inflation and of unemployment. Conservative-minded Keynesians wanted to run the economy at a slightly higher 'margin of unused capacity' in order to lower inflation. This was a possible policy deduction from *The General Theory* model. But it was condemned as immoral by the growth Keynesians, who wanted to expand demand till the last person seeking work at any single moment was employed, using incomes policy to control costs, either with the agreement of the trade unions, or by legislation. But, as Alan Coddington observed, the Keynesian habit of treating the centralization of power as a residual from the solution to problems of economic management ignored the question of how much power the government actually had, or should have in a free society. The failure of Keynesians to take supply constraints seriously, the product of the depression perspective of *The General Theory*, destroyed not only the intellectual balance which Keynes himself tried to hold, but also the political balance of the Keynesian revolution. By the late 1970s, lovers of liberty and those who valued efficiency started to desert the Keynesian camp in droves.

Keynes was less guilty of political naïvety than some of his detractors believe – he once remarked memorably that politicians have only ears not eyes – but he paid little attention to the political process by which policy is made, and therefore often gave the impression that, provided the state apparatus was equipped with the right theories and run by benevolent Old Etonians, it could be safely entrusted with much more discretionary power over economic policy than the Victorians would have considered prudent or desirable. It is easy to believe that he himself would have been more sensible and cautious in policy advice or conduct than later Keynesian economists and politicians; but it is difficult to find, either in *The General Theory*, or in other of his writings, any explicit discussion of the necessary limits which should be placed on discretionary economic action, either because the prince was inherently corrupt as the Victorians believed, or for the sake of the credibility of the policies being pursued or commitments entered into. Keynesians like Christopher Dow noticed that the 'fine tuning' interventions of British governments in the 1950s tended to be destabilizing, but attributed this to incompetence, even though it was apparent to more independent-minded observers like Terence Hutchison that governments were trying (with some success) to manipulate the economy to win elections.

More importantly, Keynesians did not suspect that inflation might be endogenous to the political process, characteristically attributing the increasingly malign outcomes of the 1970s to random shocks, avoidable errors, or the stupidity or selfishness of trade-union leaders, etc. It was left to the anti-Keynesian public choice school of economists to argue rigorously that politicians were in the business of maximizing a political utility function rather than a social welfare function, and to erect on this insight proposals for subjecting economic decision-making to constitutional or other rules. Whether the public choice theorists are right or wrong in the motives they ascribe to politicians and bureaucrats, the credibility issue has to be faced in an era of global capital markets. Unfortunately experience of Keynesian management in the 1970s has led the markets to mistrust any government which does not bind itself with hoops of steel to maintain a low rate of inflation.

The fundamental criticism of Keynes is not that his theory of output as a whole was so 'general' that it could be applied in any type of society ranging from democratic to totalitarian – something he explicitly acknowledged in the German preface to *The General Theory* – but that he never specified what types of application were appropriate to a free society and what were not. It is difficult to know from his writings, economic and political, where he would have drawn the line. He probably did not think it was necessary to do so, relying, in a very English way, on the automatic restraints of a community which 'thinks and feels rightly' to stop rulers doing dreadful things in his name.

In the light of this background, all too briefly sketched in, one can see why Keynesian policy has been in abeyance since the end of the 1970s, despite the heavy and persisting unemployment. There has been a general loss of confidence in the managerial, administrative, and spending activities of the state. The Keynesian revolution has been engulfed in a 'rhetoric of reaction', promiscuously directed at all forms of collectivism. The main political project over the more recent period has been to disinflate economies, restore public finances, de-corporatize and deregulate industrial relations, roll back (if possible) public spending, and privatize state industries. Unemployment has been viewed by the governments in power either as the necessary cost of accomplishing these reforms, or as something to be tackled after they have been accomplished. Such policies reflect the expectations formed by the Keynesian experience.

There remain fascinating questions. Could a more modest version of Keynesian policy in the 1960s have prevented the formation of expectations which made it unusable? Would Keynes himself have tried the incomes-policy route? There is no way of knowing. But it is worth remembering that Keynes was never someone to go down with a sinking ship, even one sailing under his flag. He would have tried to preserve the baby – his baby – while throwing out the bathwater.

Today, Keynesian policy cannot be openly avowed, though political pressure can still cause it to be pursued by stealth. Macroeconomic policy is increasingly pragmatic and a-theoretical. How it will evolve is uncertain. But two observations seem reasonably secure. With the globalization of markets, especially capital markets, the era of national economic management, which opened in 1914, is over. Keynesian policies, if pursued at all, will need to be on a global, or at the very least, regional basis. The era of discretionary demand management is also over. Whatever the eventual form of the policy framework it will be much more rule-bound than it was in the 1960s or 1970s. The Keynesian view of governments as benign social welfare maximizers is discredited beyond present repair. However, money supply or balanced budget rules will not be credible if the markets expect that political pressure will force them to be broken.

The question of how much Keynesianism will be needed to keep the world economy stable and prosperous in the years ahead is much harder to answer. It will partly depend on the outcome of the transition from Communism to capitalism in the former Soviet Empire and China. Will the transition usher in an era of very turbulent politics or will it reopen frontiers long closed to trade and commerce, and restore that confidence in progress and prosperity shattered by the 1914–18 war? The nature of the conjuncture will determine the governing ideas which capitalist economies will need; but the ideas will also determine the nature of the conjuncture. One cannot get away from this mutual dependence in social life. It should come as no surprise to learn that the ever-fertile mind of Keynes is a rich source of ideas directly relevant to the problems of the transition economies.

How much is left of Keynes? Keynes always insisted that economic models must be 'relevant to the contemporary world', and said of his remedies that they are 'on a different plane from my diagnosis . . . not meant to be definitive, [but] subject to all sorts of special assumptions and are necessarily related to the particular conditions of the time'.

Today there is no generally accepted model either of the macroeconomy or of the microeconomy, or of the relationship between the two. On the one side, we have the anti-Keynesian monetarism of Milton Friedman, and the 'new classical' macroeconomics, associated with Robert Lucas and Thomas Sargent – the 'radical wing of monetarism' – which deny validity to Keynesian models and power (except possibly a perverse power) to Keynesian policies. The 'new classical' macroeconomists agree with the monetarists that macroeconomic policies affect nominal, but not real, variables, and that unemployment will always gravitate to its 'natural rate'. With the monetarists they believe that the 'natural rate' of unemployment can be lowered by supply-side policies designed to improve business incentives, deregulate goods and labour markets, and privatize state-owned industries. The main analytic contribution of the new classical macroeconomists is the rational expectations hypothesis. Rational agents utilize all available relevant information in making their decisions. They make correct forecasts of the effects of announced government macroeconomic policies, the forecasts (in most rational expectations models) being based on the quantity theory of money. Expansionary (or contractionary) macroeconomic policy has no real effects even in the short run (the Phillips Curve is always vertical), since prices are immediately adjusted to the anticipated monetary conditions. The paradoxical conclusion is that Keynesian measures to lower unemployment below its 'natural rate' can achieve their promised results only by surprise, hardly a basis for usable policy. This reinforces the monetarist contention that macroeconomic policy should follow fixed rules to minimize expectational errors.

On the other side, Keynesians believe that demand matters, and that there remains a significant role for purposeful government policy in reducing unemployment. European experience of the 1980s and early 1990s bears out Keynes's contention that shocks to demand, whether coming from the private sector or the government, can lead to persisting unemployment. Why this should be so is not clearly understood. If individuals are rational optimizers, how is it that unwanted unemployment can persist when opportunities exist for mutually beneficial trade? The puzzle has belatedly given rise to a lively Keynesian research programme. The 'new Keynesians' have tried to understand the causes of rigid wages and prices, simply assumed as facts of life by the Keynesians of the 1950s. They have developed models to explain imperfect adjustment to shocks based on information costs, coordination failures, menu costs, efficiency wage hypotheses, sunspot equilibria, hysteresis, and so on. These models are designed to show that, even with rational expectation, labour markets may not clear. The Post-Keynesian school has continued to emphasize Keynes's stress on the importance of time and uncertainty, the use of money as a store of value, and the 'animal spirits' theory of investment. Conventional behaviour by capitalists or workers which produces perverse results for the economy as a whole is seen as a sensible response to uncertainty, or in the Sraffian and Kaleckian versions of Post-Keynesianism, to the class struggle.

Despite their disagreements on the role of macroeconomic policy, there is a growing agreement between all the schools, Keynesian and anti-Keynesian, that supply-side measures can lower present unemployment, either by sweeping away obstacles to market transactions or by rebuilding damaged capacity, or by a mixture of both.

The question of what, and how much, governments should *continually* do to stabilize economic activity at a high level will not disappear. The answer one gives will depend partly on what one thinks the economy is like, partly on what one thinks governments are like. If an unmanaged economy is 'inherently more cyclically stable' than Keynes thought, the answer is: not very much. The very least government should do is not make things worse. Friedman believes that most traumatic shocks are political. Governments are irretrievably tempted to manipulate the monetary parameters in order to secure helpful short-run results. Therefore their discretionary activity should be strictly circumscribed by rules. Keynes believed that unmanaged economies are inherently volatile, with a tendency to subnormal activity, so that policy can play a large part in both stabilizing and raising their performance. He thought governments could be sufficiently trusted to carry out contra-cyclical policy with competence and probity.

It is difficult to resolve this question empirically. It can certainly be argued that Keynesian policy (with all its impure political admixtures) made matters worse than they would have been from the mid-1960s onwards. But history shows that private-sector activity can be very volatile. Moreover, monetarism failed to predict the high persisting levels of European unemployment which followed the disinflationary policies of the early 1980s, and it has failed to produce a viable financial rule.

This leads to the conclusion that economics has consistently oversold itself as a 'guide to action', as opposed to an organized method of thinking about states of affairs and about the design of institutions capable of sustaining well-being beyond the actions of a particular government in a particular place at a particular time. Economists have not, in Keynes's phrase, become as useful as dentists. One cannot help reflecting that it was in the 1960s, when theoretically based macroeconomic policy was most actively used, that it started to go seriously wrong, and that it was those very prejudices and institutions which constrained the discretionary use of Keynesian tools in the 1950s which kept economic policy relatively circumspect. Eisenhower Keynesianism did more good than Kennedy Keynesianism.

If we are to draw a lesson from post-war historical experience it is that Keynesianism works best as a discretionary resource in a rule-based framework which places strong constraints on the actions of governments and which promotes the well-being of peoples through the widest possible measures of free trade. Those who look for inspiration to Keynes today are more likely to be impressed by the care and thought which he gave to the design of the Bretton Woods system than with Keynesian prescriptions for the parochial diseases of individual economies. Consciously or unconsciously we are trying to recreate the happy conjuncture which produced the 'golden age', much chastened by the experience of the intervening years. Whether we succeed will depend, in part, on the quality of statesmanship.

Epilogue: The view from 2010

When I wrote on Keynes 15 years ago, Keynes's star was fading. By common consent, the Keynesian age had collapsed in theoretical disarray and policy disorder, victim of simultaneous inflation and unemployment which Keynesian economists could not explain and Keynesian policy-makers could not control. It was in this situation that classical economics – the economics Keynes had apparently overthrown – made a big comeback, and governments reverted to a modified pre-Keynesian policy stance. Markets were deemed to be optimally self-regulating; the macroeconomic task of government was restricted to maintaining 'sound money'; government's task in the micro-economy was to free up markets in order to lower the 'natural rate of unemployment'. The revival of classical economics and its theory of economic policy was enormously helped by the fall of Communism in 1990. This made possible for the first time since 1914 the restoration of a single world economy based on balanced budgets, free trade, and unrestricted capital movements – the pre-1914 recipe for economic success. 'Globalization' was the name given to this worldwide extension of the market system.

My 1995 account of Keynes's contribution to economics was swayed by these theoretical and real-world happenings, but there was a lot of life left in my Keynes. As I wrote, 'the deflationary policies pursued over the last fifteen years have left high and persisting unemployment in their wake – as indeed Keynes predicted such policies would'. In other words, economies did not bounce back quickly to full employment and rapid growth after a shock. Events since then have brought Keynes back to more vigorous life. The so-called 'Great Moderation' after 1997/8 which seemed to vindicate the new regime of deregulated markets lasted less than ten years: from today's perspective, it resembles nothing so much as the 'roaring twenties' which preceded the Great Depression of 1929–32. With the financial collapse of 2007–8, 'new classical' belief in self-regulating markets has proved to be as illusory as the old classical belief.

My ideas of what was significant in Keynes, and his legacy, have shifted, partly because the world has changed. Below I indicate the five topics that have taken on greater significance since the first edition of the book came out.

The role of uncertainty

I would now assign a much greater weight to uncertainty in Keynes's thinking than I did in 1995. It was not that I was unaware of it. Indeed, I would not alter a word of the first paragraph of Chapter 1. But I did not place it at the heart of my account of Keynes's theory. In this, I followed the conventional treatment. The purpose of the *General Theory* was to explain how an economy could get stuck in a low employment trap, not how it had arrived there. In other words, it was an equilibrium theory.

This seemed the right model for the time, because the world wanted to know how to get out of the trap. The theory of the multiplier showed how much extra demand needed to be pumped into a depressed economy to bring it back to full employment. The income/expenditure model was thus the bit of Keynes most suitable for the policy-maker, and this was the form Keynes gave it in his great book, asides apart.

In the *General Theory* expectations were taken as given. Aggregate demand was simply expected income. Why one level of income was expected rather than another was not explained. But any theory which seeks to explain the *movement* of an economy through time requires a theory of expectations.

This is where Keynes's theory of uncertain expectations comes in. What causes economies to collapse is the existence of *uncertain* expectations. Uncertainty plays a minor part in the plot of the *General Theory*. It enters the picture only after the statement of the positive part of his theory, which assumes given expectations. Yet it is obvious, I think, that without uncertain expectations there would be no plot. The collapse of investment which drives the economy into a slump would not happen, interest rates would automatically rebalance any discrepancy between *ex ante* saving and investment, and the classical theory would be the relevant one for all circumstances. Yet what was a 'digression' in the *General Theory* became its central message when Keynes restated the 'simple fundamental ideas' which underpinned his theory in an article entitled 'The General Theory of Employment', published in the *Quarterly Journal of Economics*, February 1937. Economists like Shackle (1967), Minsky (1975), Chick (1992), and Davidson (1972, 2007) have based their interpretation of Keynes on the 1937 article.

Many commentators have argued that Keynes had little or nothing to say about financial instability. This is wrong: the instability of investment as a cause of crisis is a continuous theme in his writing (see, for example, the *Treatise on Money*); with its cause – inescapable uncertainty about the future – clearly identified. Equally clearly, Keynes identifies predictable knowledge of the future as the key tacit assumption behind the classical theory of the self-regulating market. If we knew what tomorrow would bring, there would never – assuming rational behaviour – be a financial or economic crisis.

Keynes's view that uncertain expectations are the root cause of financial crisis may be contrasted with today's conventional view that the banking collapse of 2008–9 was caused by the 'mispricing of risk'. Behind this lies the notion that risks can be correctly priced, but that markets were impeded from discovering these correct prices by information or incentive failures. The key to the prevention of further crises is therefore better 'risk managment', by the banks and by the regulators: more transparency, better risk models, and, above all, better incentives to evaluate correctly the risks being run. The argument seems to be between those who say risks are always correctly priced – the Efficient Market Hypothesis – and those who concede that imperfect information and/or the wrong incentives can cause market prices to deviate from the correct prices given by 'fundamentals'.

In contrast, Keynes made a key distinction between risk and uncertainty. Risk is when probabilities can be known (measured); uncertainty exists when they cannot be known (or measured). His original insight was that the classical theory of the self-regulating market rested on the epistemological claim that market participants have perfect information – a claim revived in the theory of rational expectations. Grant this, and the full employment assumption follows; deny it, and it collapses. Keynes's economy is one in which our knowledge of the future is 'usually very slight and often negligible' and expectations are frequently subject to disappointment. This renders the accumulation of wealth 'a peculiarly unsuitable subject for the methods of the classical economic theory'. Models which assume that we have calculable probabilities for all future contingencies are essentially fraudulent prospectuses.

What was it that rendered large parts of the future impervious to probabilistic calculation? Keynes gave the example of an apple endowed with 'human' characteristics. Newtonian physics tells us that it will always fall to the ground, at a speed dictated by the force exerted on it divided by its mass. But no such prediction can be made about the 'human' apple.

> It is as though the fall of the apple to the ground depended on the apple's motives, on whether it is worthwhile falling to the ground, and whether the ground wanted the apple to fall, and on mistaken calculations on the part of the apple on how far it was from the centre of the earth.

Some part of the uncertainty attaching to the speed of the apple's fall can be put down to mistakes on the apple's part ('mistaken calculations') which are in principle correctible. However, the main 'human' characteristics with which Keynes equips his apple are 'motives' and 'intentions'. It is these which break the link between economics and physics, and which make economics a 'moral' and not a 'natural' science. Keynes's point is that economics 'deals with introspection and values ... with motives, expectations, psychological uncertainties'. The future can't be predicted, because the future is unpredictably changeable. It is unpredictably changeable, in large part, because it is what we choose to make it. This view implies a large restriction on the applicability of econometrics. Basically, Keynes believed it could be applied only to those fields in which risk is measurable. This excluded many of the risks incurred in investment markets.

The main technique we adopt to cope with an uncertain universe is to give risk numbers. This is what mathematical forecasting models do, using some version of Bayes' theorem to transform prior into posterior probabilities. This gives us the assurance we need to invest. But it is a fake assurance. While repeated betting on horses allows you to update your 'priors' to match the 'true' merits of the horses, no amount of data on past economic events brings you any closer to their true likelihood of occurring in the future, because the future is bound to be different from the past. What we do is to use mathematics to *invent* a world of calculable probabilities which we take to be an accurate reflection of the real world.

Thinking about the future as calculable is not foolish. In fact, it is the only rational basis of individual action. It is also compatible, as Keynes notes, with a considerable measure of stability. Mathematical forecasts can shape the future they claim to predict, by shaping our expectations. They may produce what economists call 'bootstrap' equilibria, paths which are what they are not because the world is what it is, but because beliefs about the world are what they are. They tell a story about the future which gives confidence, as long as nothing happens to shake confidence in the story.

Why does investment break down? Keynes's answer is that the technique for transforming uncertainty into calculable risk is based on the convention that 'the existing state of affairs will continue indefinitely, except in so far as we have specific reasons to expect a change in the near future ... we are assuming, in effect, that the existing market valuation, however arrived at, is *uniquely* correct in relation to our existing knowledge, and that it will only change in proportion to changes in our knowledge'. This convention is philosophically flawed, 'since our existing knowledge does not provide a sufficient basis for calculated mathematical expectation'. Nevertheless, by using the convention, the investor can 'legitimately encourage himself with the idea that the only risk he runs is that of a genuine change in the news *over the near future*', which is unlikely to be very large. 'Thus investment becomes reasonably "safe" for the individual investor over short periods, and hence over a succession of short periods ... if he can fairly rely on there being no breakdown in the convention.' Keynes believed that 'it has been ... on the basis of some such procedure as this that our leading investment markets have been developed'.

The flaw in the method is that it abstracts from uncertainty by assuming that the future will be a succession of very short intervals, for each of which we can expect to have reliable information. In practice, the prospective yield (discounted future cash flow) of an investment over a number of years is subject to all kinds of unknowns about future interest rates, inflation rates, exchange rates, choice of interest rates for 'discounting', and so on. The assumption of the Efficient Market Hypothesis that all the relevant information about the future prices of securities is already contained in their current prices is as heroic as is the belief that econometric analysis will give us reliable information about the future course of microeconomic and macroeconomic variables. The first fails to explain how current prices can diverge from so-called 'intrinsic values'; the second assumes knowledge about things about which there is no scientific basis to form any calculable probability. Contrary to the current orthodoxy that expectations are realized on average, Keynes believed them to be disappointed on average, with rare moments of satisfaction. He also believed that uncertainty forced professional investment into speculation, since speed of transactions was the key to avoid being left holding the bad penny when the music stopped.

Expectations so precariously based are liable to be swept away, because, as Keynes says, 'there is no firm basis of conviction to hold them steady' – that is, to be able to distinguish between new relevant information and 'noise'. Suddenly everyone starts revising their bets.

> The practice of calmness and immobility, of certainty and security, suddenly breaks down. New fears and hopes will, without warning take charge of human conduct. The forces of disillusion may suddenly impose a new conventional basis of valuation. All these pretty, polite techniques, made for a well panelled board room and a nicely regulated market, are liable to collapse.

This is as good a theoretical explanation as I know of for the meltdown in the autumn of 2008.

However, the story is only half told. Investment depends on what Keynes calls the marginal efficiency of capital (MEC) – roughly, the expected rate of return over cost – as compared to the rate of interest. If MEC is greater than the rate of interest, investment takes place; if less, it falls. In the classical picture, the rate of interest, being the price that equilibrates saving and investment, adjusts automatically to any change in the MEC. Keynes accepted that the volume of investment depends on the rate of interest, but denied that the rate of interest was determined in the market for saving and investment. Rather, it is the price for parting with money. This is his liquidity-preference theory of the rate of interest. Money plays a key part in Keynes's narrative of investment breakdown. Holding money is an alternative to buying investments. Keynes was the first economist who clearly identified the role of money as a 'store of value'. What he called 'liquidity preference' rises when the 'convention' supporting investment collapses. A rise in liquidity preference can retard the fall in the rate of interest necessary to bring about a recovery of investment in face of a fall in expected profitability. Indeed, a fall in the expected profitability of investment and a flight into money are two sides of the the same coin. This is essentially what happened in 2007–8. Liquidity suddenly dried up as banks enlarged their cash balances and stopped lending. Indebtedness played a larger part in the freeze-up than it did during the time of the Great Depression, but the essential motive for the flight into money – loss of confidence in the future – was the same. The rise in liquidity-preference when the MEC collapses is Keynes's main explanation of why the market system lacks an automatic correction mechanism.

Keynes's equilibrium method also cut him off from a theoretical explanation of how involuntary unemployment comes about. It is defined as a situation in which there are more people willing to work for a lower real wage than there are employed. The question then is: why does not competition between workers bid down real wages sufficiently for all to find jobs? Or to put it another way: how can Keynes's under-employment equilibrium be a real equilibrium if it contains disequilibrium prices? A major theoretical weakness of the post-war Keynesians was their inability to explain persisting unemployment except in terms of 'sticky' wages, and their inability to explain why wages were sticky. Axel Leijonhufvud goes some way to filling this theoretical gap within a (non-Keynesian) theory of long-period full employment. As he points out, the main innovation of the *General Theory* was to create a model in which the system reacts to a disturbance by quantity not price adjustments. Following a shock, output and prices both adjust. But prices adjust slower than output because people don't know what the new equilibrium price is. So they trade at disequilibrium prices. There is no auctioneer to establish a 'vector of market clearing prices' before trade starts. Further, only in the very long run need long-term interest rates conform to underlying physical transformation possibilities and inter-temporal household preferences. Uncertainty may thus cause real wages and long-term interest rates to remain for years above the rates needed for full employment.

The debate about the stimulus

When the financial system crashed in 2008, dragging down the real economy with it, governments stepped in everywhere with 'stimulus packages' made up of a mixture of printing money, providing tax rebates or subsidies for private spending, and big increases in loan-financed public spending. This was all according to Keynesian prescription. Even Robert Lucas, high priest of Chicago economics, admitted that 'we are all Keynesians in the foxhole'. But signs of economic recovery rapidly brought about a resumption of normal intellectual service. Most economists and many policy-makers are calling for a swift withdrawal of the stimulus on the ground that it will bankrupt governments or lead to inflation or both. What this rapid turnabout shows is that the model of the economy which Keynes had tried to blast out of the minds of economists in the early 1930s is still firmly lodged there. It wavers in moments of panic, but quickly reasserts itself. In fact, the current debate about the stimulus is a replay of the debate between Keynes and his critics at the time of the Great Depression.

In 1929, with British unemployment standing at 10% of the insured workforce, Keynes and Hubert Henderson wrote a pamphlet entitled *Can Lloyd George Do It?* In this, they proposed a big programme of public works, to be financed by loan, to induce a 'cumulative wave of prosperity'. The British Treasury attempted to refute the proposal using an argument developed by its then only economist, R. G. Hawtrey. Hawtrey had claimed that, with a fixed money supply, any loan raised by the government for public works would 'crowd out' an equivalent amount of private spending. Employment could be increased only by credit expansion – or what was then called inflation. The prime minister, Stanley Baldwin, was fed the lines 'we must *either* take existing money *or* create new money'.

Keynes riposted: 'Mr. Baldwin has invented the formidable argument that you must not do anything because it means you will not be able to do anything else.' Yet the Treasury argument of 1929 was restated in 2009 in almost identical terms by Professor John Cochrane of Chicago University:

> If money is not going to be printed, it has to come from somewhere. If the government borrows a dollar from you, that is a dollar that you do not spend, or that you do not lend to a company to spend on new investment. Every dollar of increased government spending must correspond to one less dollar of private spending. Jobs created by stimulus spending are offset by jobs from the decline of private spending. We can build roads instead of factories, but fiscal stimulus can't help us to build more of both.

The policy implication of this argument is that the fiscal stimulus was a mistake and should be withdrawn as soon as possible in order to create room for private spending. And this has been the almost unanimous call of conservative politicians and commentators. This call would be correct if the economy were at full employment. But coming at a point when production and employment had fallen by 5%, it was plainly nonsensical. Government spending to put the unemployed to work is not taking away employment from those already in work: it is adding to the amount of employment. It is equally obvious that increased government spending will have to be financed initially by printing money, because any fall in aggregate spending will have led to a collapse in the money supply. But as the new money is spent, there will be extra dollars for the government to borrow without 'taking it away' from the owners of existing dollars. Keynes explained all this clearly in 1937, when he pointed out that an investment decision may involve 'a temporary demand for money... before the corresponding saving has taken place'. Thus, though extra investment (private or public) could not be limited by a 'shortage of saving', it could exceed the supply of financial facilities 'if the banking system is unwilling to increase the supply of money and the supply from existing holders [of inactive balances] is inelastic'. In this situation, the central bank could always create the 'finance' for additional investment, private or public, by printing more money. If the investment takes place, 'the appropriate level of incomes will be generated out of which there will necessarily remain over an amount of saving exactly sufficient to take care of the new investment'.

Contemporary Hawtreyans argue that printing money is a necessary and sufficient condition for a revival of private spending. There is no need for extra government spending on public works and so on. When the central bank buys government and corporate securities, it adds to the cash reserves of banks and companies. These purchases enable banks to expand their deposits (loans) and companies to expand their investments. Thus, 'open-market operations', carried out to any extent necessary, will be sufficient to produce recovery from even a severe slump.

Keynes certainly believed something like this when he wrote the *Treatise on Money* in 1929–30. Monetary policy, he thought, would be sufficient to rescue an economy from a slump except in the exceptional circumstance when the expectation of profit had fallen below the minimum interest rates at which banks were prepared to lend. By 1932, he thought this circumstance had come to pass. 'It may still be the case', he said in his Halley-Stewart lecture of 4 February 1932,

> that the lender, with his confidence shattered by his experience, will continue to ask for new enterprise rates of interest which the borrower cannot expect to earn ... If this proves to be the case there will be no means of escape from prolonged and perhaps interminable depression except by direct state intervention to promote and subsidise new investment.

The long Japanese stagnation of the 1990s brought into prominence the idea of a 'liquidity trap'. Keynes asked: why someone should hold money for any purpose other than the transactions and precautionary motives, when he could obtain an income by investing it in bonds? Keynes found that the necessary condition for such speculative money-holding is 'the existence of *uncertainty* as to the future rate of interest'. If the rates of interest ruling in future could be foreseen with certainty, 'it must always be more advantageous to purchase a debt than to hold cash as a store of wealth'. However, if the future rates of interest were uncertain, the outcome could be quite different. If interest rates rise, a capital loss is suffered, with the loss being higher the more long-dated is the bond. Keynes warned that, for an investor thinking of acquiring a bond with a life of n years, ' ... if a need for liquid cash may conceivably arise before the expiry of n years, there is a risk of loss being incurred in purchasing a long-term debt and subsequently turning it into cash, as compared with holding cash'. Keynes's conclusion was that, when there were enough investors who expected the next move in interest rates to be upwards, they would hold at least part of their wealth in the form of money rather than bonds. They would do this even if they would be foregoing income in the immediate future. In the extreme – when bond yields had fallen so low that the only sensible expectation was a future rise in the bond yield (i.e., the only sensible expectation was a capital loss) – investors would keep idle any extra money balances that might be injected into their portfolios. The economy would be in a liquidity trap: people would accumulate money balances without limit. Open-market operations could not rescue it. Only fiscal policy could. Keynes did not believe that a pure liquidity trap – in the sense that the LM curve is flat – had ever arisen, though the United States in the 1930s had come close to it. But clearly any flattening of the LM curve, even if short of a trap, reduces the effectiveness of monetary policy. Keynes did not worry too much about the trap, since, if it happened, while monetary policy would be disabled, the government would be able to borrow unlimited amounts at a nominal rate of interest for its own spending.

Keynes's liquidity trap discussion has been heavily criticized for being analytically incomplete. He postulated only two alternatives – holding cash or buying bonds. But savers may express their desire for liquidity by increasing their demand for other liquid assets such as equities. If investors have a choice between money, bonds, and equities, and one allows for the increase in money to alter inflation expectations, Keynes's trap disintegrates. However, this does not, it seems to me, rescue the case for monetary policy as a sufficient cure for a slump. Quantitative easing has undoubtedly had a positive effect on stock market prices. But most of it has not yet (at the time of writing, February 2010) filtered into the real economy. It has bid up prices of existing assets, but not stimulated new investment, because lenders are still asking more from borrowers than borrowers can expect to earn. The general proposition is that the emergence of asset bubbles, just as much as a flight into money, can signal a dearth of investment opportunities. Keynes's 'speculative motive' for holding money should not be confused with the desire for cash alone.

Global imbalances

Keynes's 1941 plan for an international clearing union was designed to overcome the global imbalances of his day, namely the blocking of balance of payments adjustment by the tendency of the United States to accumulate gold reserves, which imposed deflation on the rest of the world. Recent years have seen East Asia and the Middle East start on their process of reserve accumulation.

Keynes's perspective on global imbalances was formed not just by the disturbances of the interwar years but by his reading of monetary history. He thought that throughout history the desire to hoard savings had been stronger than the desire to invest them, because at all times vague fears lie below the surface, denting our optimism, and creating a permanent bias towards preserving existing value rather than creating new value. This was his explanation of why the world had stayed poor for so long. He believed that investment came in bursts of optimism, which he called 'animal spirits'. We can trace these investment upsurges in history – from the railway boom of the 19th century to the dot.com boom which ended in 2000. But normally people preferred to hoard rather than invest their money, that is to say, there was a permanently high level of liquidity preference which exerted a permanent upward pressure on interest rates. Hence, Keynes's support for the medieval usury laws, which he saw as an attempt to prevent people making money by hoarding money.

Keynes's theory of economic history was influenced by Jevons's famous description of India as the 'sink of the precious metals'. 'The history of India at all times', he wrote in the *General Theory*,

> has provided an example of a country impoverished by a preference
> for liquidity amounting to so strong a passion that even an
> enormous and chronic influx of the precious metals has been

insufficient to bring down the rate of interest to a level which was compatible with the growth of real wealth.

Keynes believed that from ancient times onwards, the Orient's propensity to hoard influxes of the precious metals had set the Occident a permanent deflationary problem. Shortage of gold in the West had been relieved from time to time by discoveries of gold and silver in the New World, and by Western seizure of Oriental temple and palace hoards.

Keynes would thus have seen the global imbalances of today as the reappearance of an ancient pattern, though with a modern twist.

In a system of floating exchange rates, balance of payments adjustment is, in theory, automatic: movements in the exchange rates of currencies correct any imbalance in trade flows. This is as true of a gold standard (in which domestic currencies are convertible into gold) as of a fiduciary standard. The situation is more complicated when countries are committed to allowing their currencies to be freely converted into gold at a fixed rate. In this case, a country running a current account deficit cannot devalue its currency in terms of gold: it has to deflate its domestic prices. By contrast, the country gaining gold has the option to inflate its domestic prices, 'hoard' (sterilize) its accumulating gold, or make foreign loans. This is what led Keynes to write in 1941:

> the process of adjustment is *compulsory* for the debtor and *voluntary* for the creditor. If the creditor does not choose to make, or allow, his share of the adjustment, he suffers no inconvenience. For whilst a country's reserve cannot fall below zero, there is no ceiling which sets an upper limit. The same is true if international loans are to be the means of adjustment. The debtor *must* borrow; the creditor is under no ... compulsion [to lend].

The deficit country deflates its domestic prices (or costs of production) by raising interest rates; whence, in Keynes's view, unemployment. For, as he wrote in 1925, the policy of credit restriction to lower prices can only attain its end *'by the deliberate intensification of unemployment'*. The chief 'hoarder' in the interwar years was the United States, whose super-competitive position, fortified by an undervalued exchange rate, enabled it to drain gold from the rest of the system, including Britain.

Keynes's Clearing Union plan of 1941 was designed to retain the advantages (as he saw them) of a fixed exchange rate system while avoiding the asymmetric costs of adjustment. As I explain on p. 113 of this volume, the essential feature of the Keynes plan was that creditor countries would not be allowed to 'hoard' their surpluses, or charge punitive rates of interest for lending them out; rather, these surpluses would be automatically available as cheap overdraft facilities to debtors through the mechanism of an international clearing bank whose depositors were the central banks of the union. The Keynes plan was vetoed by the United States, which was not prepared to allow its 'hard-earned' surpluses to be automatically placed at the disposal of 'profligate' debtor countries. Instead, the Bretton Woods Agreement of 1944 set up an International Monetary Fund to provide short-term financial assistance, on conditions, for countries in temporary balance of payments difficulties. But the onus still lay on the debtor country to deflate its wages and prices to restore balance of payments equilibrium.

That the Bretton Woods fixed exchange rate system, which lasted from 1949 to 1971, did not reproduce the deflationary character of the interwar system was entirely due to the 'dishoarding' policies of the United States. America flooded the 'free' world with dollars, to such an extent that by the 1960s it was starting to run a balance of trade deficit itself. The boot was now, so to speak, on the other foot, but the logic of the deficit country having to deflate was circumvented by the fact that the dollar became the world's chief reserve asset. In his book *Indian Currency and Finance* (1913), Keynes had endorsed the gold exchange standard as being in the forefront of monetary evolution. Broadly speaking, it envisaged one or two countries only staying on the gold standard, with the rest of the world holding their reserves in these currencies, which because of their convertibility into gold would be 'as good as gold'. As sterling faded, the dollar became the world's sole 'key' currency. As its trade deficit widened, the United States printed an increasing quantity of dollars to cover its unrequited imports. The surplus countries accumulated American dollar liabilities which they invested in US Treasury bonds. The United States did not have to restrict domestic credit by raising interest rates since the dollars it printed came back to it. In the absence of what would have been a major deflationary force, the world economy boomed for twenty years.

The flaw in the system, as pointed out by Professor Triffin of Yale University, was that the increase in the liabilities of the key-currency country was bound to raise doubts about its ability to redeem these liabilities in gold. This brought about the predicted collapse of the gold-exchange standard in 1971. The dollar became inconvertible, and a new international reserve currency, the IMF's Special Drawing Rights (SDRs), was set up. But without the essential element of conversion of dollar balances into SDRs, the dollar continued to be the world's main reserve currency in a mixed world of floating, fixed, and managed exchange rates.

In the 1990s, the need for reserves unexpectedly revived, mainly to guard against speculative movements of hot money which could drive exchange rates away from their equilibrium values. Starting in the 1990s, East Asian governments unilaterally erected a 'Bretton Woods II', linking their currencies to the dollar, and holding their reserves in dollars. This reproduced the expansionary benefits of Bretton Woods I, but at the cost of an increasingly unbalanced reserve position, as the dollar became progressively overvalued against the super-competitive renmimbi.

A Keynesian analysis would put the global imbalances at the heart of the current economic meltdown. Keynesian unemployment is triggered off by an imbalance between saving and investment which is liquidated by a fall in output. The imbalance can be initiated either by an increased desire to save or a reduced desire to invest, or by a mixture of both. Assume a closed economy, as Keynes did in the *General Theory*. And then postulate the following: an increased desire to save (by the Chinese) unmatched by an increased US desire to invest subjects the US economy to deflationary pressure. This was offset by an inflow of dollars invested in US Treasuries, which enabled Alan Greenspan to keep the Fed funds rate abnormally low. But the ensuing credit expansion resulted not in a surge in investment but the build-up of a debt-fuelled private asset and consumption boom. The situation was unsustainable because no new resources were being created with which to pay back either domestic or foreign borrowing. Between June 2004 and July 2006, the Federal Reserve, seeking to dampen inflation and return short-term interest rates to a more normal level, raised the federal funds rate from 1% to 5.25%, and held it there until August 2007. This brought about a collapse in the housing boom, and through its repercussions on the balance sheet of the banks which had provided or securitized housing mortgages, of the banking system. As Keynes explained in his account of Britain's 1914 banking crisis: 'If A owes B money, and B owes it to C, and C to D, and so on, the failure of A may involve the failure of the whole series.'

This is not unlike what happened at the end of the 1920s. Judged by commodity prices, there was no danger of US inflation in 1927. Hence, by raising its funds rate from 3.5% to 5% in July 1928, the Fed was imposing an act of deflation on the US economy. As Keynes wrote in October 1928:

> I cannot help feeling that the risk just now is all on the side of a
> business depression and deflation . . . If too prolonged an attempt is
> made to check the speculative position by dear money, it may well be

that the dear money, by checking new investments, will bring about a general business depression.

This is essentially what I believe happened in 2007–8.

Keynes's political economy

At present, the reform agenda for averting future crises concentrates entirely on reforming or restructuring the banking system to prevent imprudent lending. These reforms are very necessary. But there is a common assumption that once the crisis is over, macroeconomic policy can continue as before – that is, with a single target: the inflation rate. However, there will continue to exist many risks which cannot be properly managed because they are unmeasurable. So part of the risk-reduction role has to be assumed by the government. This implies an extension of the macroeconomic functions of government.

Keynes's recipe for a less uncertain economy consisted of three main elements: measures to stimulate investment, measures to stimulate consumption, and a reform of the international monetary system to prevent the transmission of unemployment from one country to another.

The first duty of the state is to ensure enough investment in the economy to maintain continuous full employment. Although cutting taxes might give a temporary boost to investment, it will have only a weak and uncertain effect on profit expectations. For the same reason, Keynes doubted the success of a purely monetary policy in maintaining a full employment level of investment. The ground for this scepticism has already been explained. The attempt by the monetary authority to reduce long-term interest rates to below the rate the market considers (from historical experience) to be the 'safe' or 'normal' rate, by inducing people to sell bonds for cash, 'is perhaps the chief obstacle to a fall in the rate of interest to a very low level'. The problem of maintaining full employment thus arises from 'the association of a conventional and fairly stable long-term rate of interest with a fickle and highly unstable marginal efficiency of capital'. Keynes's solution to the problem is to use monetary policy to establish a permanently low long-term rate of interest. For '*any* level of interest which is accepted with sufficient conviction as likely to be durable *will* be durable ...'. For this reason, he did not want to use interest rates to manage the business cycle: the exact opposite of present practice. Nevertheless, he believed that it 'seems likely that the fluctuations in ... the marginal efficiency of capital ... will be too great to be offset by any practicable changes in the rate of interest'. Hence, apart from keeping interest rates permanently low, investment needed to be 'socialized'. Keynes wrote: 'I expect to see the State ... taking an ever greater responsibility for directly organising investment' and 'I conceive, therefore, that a somewhat comprehensive socialisation of investment will prove the only means of securing an approximation to full employment'.

By 'socialization of investment', Keynes did not mean nationalization. Socialization of investment need not exclude 'all manner of compromise and devices by which public authority will co-operate with private initiative'. This single throwaway line in the *General Theory* reflects Keynes's thinking on 'public–private partnerships' which came out of his involvement in Liberal politics in the 1920s. In essence, he sought to expand the public-utility component of investment to give greater stability to the investment function. Today, he would have seen the big institutional investors like pension funds as a major support for stability. A steady stream of publicly inspired investment would reduce fluctuations to modest dimensions, which could be readily controlled, if so wished, by speeding up or slowing down elements in the investment programme. Such investment would not necessarily be profit-maximizing. But provided it yielded positive returns, there would be a gain. If markets had perfect information, public investment would be inefficient. But with uncertainty, there is a gain as against having no state investment at all, because of the losses due to uncertainty.

Keynes's political economy would also have used the taxation system to stimulate private consumption, since an 'increase in the habitual tendency to consume will in general [i.e., except in conditions of full employment] serve to increase the inducement to invest'. The rationale for this is that the poor spend a higher proportion of their incomes than do the rich. Marriner Eccles, chairman of the US Federal Reserve Board from 1934 to 1948, spelled out the logic of this position better than Keynes managed himself:

> A mass production economy has to be accompanied by mass consumption. Mass consumption in turn implies a distribution of wealth to provide men with buying power. Instead of achieving that kind of distribution, a giant suction pump had by 1929 drawn into a few hands an increasing proportion of currently produced wealth. This served them as a capital accumulation. But by taking purchasing power out of the hands of mass consumers, the savers denied to themselves the kind of effective demand for their products that would justify a reinvestment of their capital accumulations in new plants. In consequence, as in a poker game when the chips were concentrated in fewer and fewer hands, the other fellows could stay in the game only by borrowing. When their credit ran out, the game stopped.

The same 'suction pump' was in operation in Britain and the United States in the run-up to the 2007 crisis, access to credit compensating for the growing inequality of wealth and incomes.

Finally, Keynes would have wanted a major reform of the international monetary system. The chief need is to reduce the amount of global reserves. Between 2003 and 2009, measurable global reserves have increased from $2.6 trillion to $6.8 trillion – an average annual rate of increase of about 15% at a time when global GDP grew at an annual rate of 4.4%. In 2003, global gold reserves amounted to 7% of total reserves; in 2009, the figure was 12%.

This flight into liquidity amounts to a large increase in deflationary pressure. Reserves are a way of insuring against uncertainty. What is required is to lower the cost of insurance by reducing uncertainty. A package of measures to achieve this would need to include internationalization of reserves, controls on hot money flows, and agreement on exchange rates.

China has proposed creating a 'super-sovereign reserve currency', but without any detail. The first step has to be funding of existing dollar holdings through the issue of SDRs. There is a precedent here in the proposal for IMF funding of the sterling balances, which Britain rejected in 1944, only to accept in 1978 in a move which finally wound up the sterling area. Agreement would be needed on the rate of future creation of IMF resources, and the terms on which they would be lent out. In conjunction with a 'Tobin' tax or quantitative controls on short-term financial transactions, these measures would greatly reduce the need to hold such large reserves. But there also needs to be agreement on exchange rates. Large swings in currency values much unjustified by changes in competitive conditions is a major cause of uncertainty in today's world. In short, we need a return to elements of the rejected Keynes Plan of 1941. Keynes would have said that unless the global monetary system is fixed, there will be a return to protection, and globalization will recede.

Towards a new economics

Keynes claimed his theory was more 'general' than classical economics because it encompassed a variety of economic situations exhibiting different states of knowledge. The question is: how central is the Keynes case? If the capitalist growth engine is subject to genuine ontological indeterminacy, then its mediocre performance and frequent breakdowns are explained. If, on the other hand, uncertainty can be plausibly modelled as an information problem, to be overcome by learning and by more efficient data processing, then Keynes's case is marginalized, and the classical theory is reinstated as the central case. The comeback of classical economics consisted in marginalizing the Keynes case, and reinserting its own theory of the self-regulating market based on 'perfect information' as the 'general case'. The breakdown of the self-regulating market in 2007–8 suggests to me that Keynes's theory is the 'general' one. But what would an economics that takes uncertainty seriously look like?

The fundamental issue involves the role of maths in economics. The older generation of economists used maths for a strictly limited purpose: to make more precise their intuitions about the real world, not to create an axiomatic system whose virtue lay in its unrealism. There has to be a return to an economics that allows room for important observations of economic behaviour which cannot be expressed in maths. Keynes himself was hostile to exaggerated precision: whether or not he was the author of the phrase 'it is better to be vaguely right than precisely wrong', this summed up his own approach. It remains to work out the teaching of economics, the production of economic textbooks, and the professional standards of economic journals to reflect these principles.

Conclusion

One clear conclusion emerges from this brief epilogue: that is, the need for a greater role for government in the management of the economy. A greater role for government in turn requires the intellectual rehabilitation of the state as a potentially rational economic actor, rather than a mere vote-seeker. It is decades since anyone was able to write, as Keynes did in 1936, of the state being 'in a position to calculate the marginal efficiency of capital-goods on long views and on the basis of the general social advantage'. We need to think about a structure of the state which allows its investment function to be separated from the political incentives facing politicians.

We do not need a new Keynes; we do need the old Keynes, suitably updated. He will not be our sole guide to the economic future, but he remains an indispensable guide.

References

Note on abbreviations

Keynes's economic writings, including all his books, many of his published essays and articles, and a large proportion of his hitherto unpublished correspondence, have been published in thirty volumes by Macmillan in conjunction with the Royal Economic Society as *The Collected Writings of John Maynard Keynes* (1971–89), ed. Elizabeth Johnson and Donald Moggridge. Most of his private papers remain unpublished and, together with the originals of the published materials in the *Collected Writings*, are deposited at King's College, Cambridge. The following abbreviations are used for Keynes's work:

CW	*The Collected Writings of John Maynard Keynes*
GT	*The General Theory of Employment, Interest, and Money*
KP	Keynes Papers
Rymes	*Keynes's Lectures, 1932–35*: notes of a representative student, transcribed, edited, and constructed by Thomas K. Rymes (1989)

Introduction

CW vii. 235
CW xxi. 244
KP, PP/57, JMK to Sterling P. Lamprecht, 19 June 1940
CW x. 447
CW x. 173–4
CW xx. 83–4

CW x. 108

CW xiv. 296–7

CW x. 365

CW xvii. 392–3

CW xxix. 166–7

The Diary of Beatrice Webb, ed. N. and J. McKenzie, iv (1985), 19 June 1936, 371.

Russell Leffingwell: Lamont Papers, Harvard University, File 103–15, Russell Leffingwell to Thomas Lamont, 29 August 1931.

J. Meade: in D. Worswick and J. Trevithick (eds.), *Keynes and the Modern World* (1983), 266.

D. Bensusan-Butt, *On Economic Knowledge* (1980), 35.

L. Tarshis, 'The Keynesian Revolution: What it Meant in the 1930s', unpublished.

O. T. Falk, 'The Tuesday Club', 23 May 1950, unpublished.

The Diary of Virginia Woolf, ed. A. O. Bell, iv (1982), 19 April 1934, 208.

B. Russell, *Autobiography* (1967), i. 72.

K. Clark, *The Other Half: A Self-Portrait* (1977), 27.

K. Martin, in *New Statesman and Nation* (28 October 1933).

K. Singer, 'Recollections of Keynes', *Australian Quarterly* (June 1949), 50–1.

Diary of Virginia Woolf, ed. Bell, iv, 12 August 1934, 236–7; iii, 21 April 1928, 181.

Walter Stewart: Clay Papers, Nuffield College, Oxford, Box 62, W. Stewart to J. Marshall, 16 May 1949.

H. Stein, *The Fiscal Revolution in America* (1969), 147–8.

Singer, 'Recollections of Keynes', 50.

N. Davenport, *Memoirs of a City Radical* (1974), 50.

Pigou and Schumpeter: see J. Cunningham Wood (ed.), *John Maynard Keynes: Critical Assessments*, ii (1983), 22, 125, respectively.

A. Marshall, *Principles of Economics* (8th edn. 1920), 85.

Singer, 'Recollections of Keynes', 55–6.

Chapter 1

CW ii. 6

CW x. 436–7

CW ii. 186

CW ix. 267

CW xxi. 233–46

CW xxi. 384–95

KP, W/1, JMK to Sheppard, 14 August 1940

Singer, 'Recollections of Keynes', 52.

H. M. Robertson, 'J. M. Keynes and Cambridge in the 1920s', *South African Journal of Economics* (September 1983), 407.

F. A. Hayek, 'A Rejoinder', *Economica* (November 1931), 401.

Letter from A. C. Gilpin to author, 22 May 1993.

Chapter 2

KP, UA/26, 'Egoism', 1906

KP, UA/21, 'Miscellanea Ethica', 1905

KP, UA/35, 'On the Principle of Organic Unity', 1910, 1921

CW xxi. 242

CW x. 445

KP, UA/19, 'Ethics in Relation to Conduct', 1904

CW viii. 32

CW viii. 356

CW viii. 348

CW x. 338–9

KP, UA/20, 'The Political Doctrines of Edmund Burke'

KP, PS/6, 1925/6

CW ix. 272–94

CW ix. 296–7

KP, PS/4

CW ix. 297

KP, PS/4

CW ix. 295–6

CW ix. 321–32

G. E. Moore, *Principia Ethica* (1903; paperback edn. 1959), 188. Ibid. 189.

Keynes's paper read to the Apostles, 23 January 1904: date supplied from the record of meetings of the Apostles by Geoffrey Lloyd, then Fellow and Tutor of King's College, Cambridge; subsequently confirmed by Dr Roderick O'Donnell.

See R. M. O'Donnell, *Keynes: Philosophy, Economics, and Politics* (1989); A. M. Carabelli, *On Keynes's Method* (1988). A. Fitzgibbons, *Keynes's Vision* (1988).

P. Clarke, 'The Politics of Keynesian Economics 1924–1931', in M. Bentley and J. Stevenson (eds.), *High and Low Politics in Modern Britain* (1983), 177–9.

M. Freeden, *Liberalism Divided* (1986), 166–71.

Keynes on Baldwin: *The Diary of Beatrice Webb*, ed. N. and
    J. McKenzie (1985), 19 June 1936, 370–1; see also
    A. L. Rowse, *Mr Keynes and the Labour Movement* (1936).

Cannan Papers, London School of Economics, Box 20c.

Bank of England spokesman: Macmillan Committee on Finance and
    Industry, Minutes of Evidence, Cmd. 2897, vol. 2, Qs. 7690–7847.

Ibid. Qs. 5565, 5650, 5654, 5684–6, 6500–24.

Chapter 3

CW xii. 701–2, 730–1

CW xii. 760

CW xii. 696

CW xii. 715–7, 730–1, 761

CW xi. 377

CW xii. 706–7

CW xii. 764

CW i. 71, 51

CW xiii. 2–14

CW ii. 148

CW iv. 36

CW iv. 126

CW iv. 139–40

CW iv. 147

CW iv. 158–60

CW iv. 146, 148

CW iv. 65

CW iv. 68

CW iv. 144

CW iv. 69

CW xix. 762

CW xiii. 273

CW ix. 115–25

CW vi. 132

CW v. 121

CW v, ch. 18

CW vi, 'Historical Illustrations'

CW v. 158–60

CW vi. 299

CW vi. 304

CW xx. 99–132
CW xiii. 178
Hawtrey Papers, Churchill College, Cambridge, 11/3, para. 22.
D. H. Robertson, *Economic Journal* (September 1931), 407.

Chapter 4

CW vii. 30
CW vi, p. xxii
CW xxi. 59–60
CW xiii. 146
CW xiii. 275–6
CW xxix. 40
Rymes, 50–3, 85–93
Rymes, 126
Rymes, 66–7, 70
CW xiii. 405
Rymes, 123–7
Rymes, 78
Rymes, 122
Rymes, 112–13
CW xxix. 57, 395–6
CW ix. 347
Rymes, 102
CW xxix. 82; Rymes, 92
CW vii. 27
CW vii. 210
CW vii. 149
CW vii. 150, 161–3
CW vii. 163–4
CW xiv. 116
CW vii. 168, 201
CW vii. 202, 203, 207–8
CW vii. 268
CW vii. 15
CW vii. 300
CW vii. 394–412
CW vii. 180
CW vii. 181
CW vii. 263
CW xxix. 179, 180

CW vii. 307

CW xxix. 87

Jens Warming: N. Cain, 'Cambridge and its Revolution', *Economic Record* (1979), 113.

D. Champernowne, in R. Lekachman (ed.), *Keynes's General Theory: A Report of Three Decades* (1964), 55–60.

D. H. Robertson, 'Some Notes on Mr. Keynes' General Theory of Employment', *Quarterly Journal of Economics* (November 1936); reprinted in J. Cunningham Wood (ed.), *John Maynard Keynes: Critical Assessments* (1983), 99–111.

J. R. Hicks, 'Mr. Keynes and the "Classics": A Suggested Interpretation', *Econometrica* (April 1937); reprinted in Cunningham Wood (ed.), *Keynes: Critical Assessments*, 162–72.

Chapter 5

CW ix. 379–80

CW xxii. 218

CW xxii. 122–3

CW xxii. 155

CW xxi. 17

CW xxi. 236

KP, L/36

CW xxv. 2

CW xxv. 15

CW xxv. 17

CW xxv. 21–40

CW xxv. 55–7

CW xxv. 156

CW xxvi. 9–21

CW xxv. 69–70

CW xxiv. 330

CW xxiv. 620, 624

D. Moggridge, *Maynard Keynes: An Economist's Biography* (1992), 631.

J. Tomlinson, *Employment Policy: The Crucial Years 1939–1955* (1987), 24.

C. H. Rolph, *Kingsley: The Life, Letters, and Diaries of Kingsley Martin* (1973), 203.

Frankfurter Papers, Library of Congress, Reel 66.

W. Carr, 'Keynes and the Treaty of Versailles', in A. P. Thirlwall (ed.), *Keynes as a Policy Adviser* (1982), 103–6.

For details of Walther Funk, see A. van Dormael, *Bretton Woods: The Birth of a Monetary System* (1978), 6–7.

Keynes's visit to USA: see E. Playfair to S. G. Waley, 16 May 1941, in Moggridge, *Keynes*, 657.

James Meade: S. Howson and D. Moggridge (eds.), *The Wartime Diaries of Leonel Robbins and James Meade 1943–1945* (1990), 106, 159, 133.

H. Dalton, *High Tide and After* (1960), 73–4.

Chapter 6

CW xxvii. 384

CW vii. 307

CW ix. 350

CW vii. 378

CW vii. 129

CW iv. 37

CW vii. 6

CW xxvii. 3

CW ii. 235–6

CW xvii. 184–5

CW vii. 296

CW vii. 302

CW xxvi. 38

CW xxvii. 385

CW vii, p. xxvi

CW xxvii. 387–8

CW xviii. 394

CW xiv. 296)

CW xiv. 122

'Students in the 1960s'; D. Worswick and J. Trevithick (eds.), *Keynes and the Modern World* (1983), 127.

Callaghan at the Labour Party Conference: see W. Grant and S. Nath, *The Politics of Economic Policy Making* (1984), 144.

Christopher Allsopp: in D. Helm (ed.), *The Economic Borders of the State* (1989), 182.

Tomlinson, *Employment Policy*, 108.

R. C. O. Matthews, 'Why Has Britain Had Full Employment since the War?', *Economic Journal* (September 1968); reprinted in Charles Feinstein (ed.), *The Managed Economy* (1983), 119.

N. F. R. Crafts and N. Woodward (eds.), *The British Economy since 1945* (1991), 7–8.

J. R. Hicks, *The Crisis in Keynesian Economics* (1974), 3.

J. Tobin, 'The Intellectual Revolution in US Economic Policy-Making', University of Essex Noel Buxton Lecture (1966).

Richard Kahn: in D. Worswick (ed.), *The Concept and Measurement of Involuntary Unemployment* (1976), 23, 27.

A. Coddington, *Keynesian Economics: The Search for First Principles* (1983), 42.

J. C. R. Dow, *The Management of the British Economy 1945–1960* (1970), 384.

T. Hutchison, *Economics and Economics Policy in Britain 1946–1966* (1968), 121–2.

Epilogue

CW xiv. 109–23
CW vi. 322–4
CW xiv. 112
CW vii. 293
CW vii. 194, 293–4
CW xiv. 113
CW xiv. 300
CW vii. 152–3
CW xiv. 114–15
CW vii. 15
CW xiv. 207–10
CW vi. 332–5
CW vii. 167–9
CW vii. 201
CW vii. 207–8
CW vii. 337
CW xxv. 28
CW ix. 220
CW xi. 241
CW xiii. 71–2
CW vii. 164
CW vii. 202

Keynes

CW vii. 204

CW vii. 203

CW vii. 164

CW vii. 378

CW vii. 378

CW vii. 373

CW vii. 164

CW xxi. 60

Axel Leijonhufvud, *Keynes and the Classics* (1969)

John Cochrane, 'Fiscal Stimulus, Fiscal Inflation, or Fiscal Fallacies?',
27 February 2009: <http//:faculty.chicagobooth.edu/john.co-
chrane/research/Papers/fiscal2.htm>, accessed 20 April 2010.

Robert Skidelsky, *The Economist as Saviour* (1992, chapters 7 and 8).

Marriner Eccles, quoted in Sam Whister (ed.), *Reforming the City*
(2009), p. 98.

Further reading

Biography

There have been five biographers of Keynes: Roy Harrod, *The Life of John Maynard Keynes* (1951); Charles Hession, *John Maynard Keynes* (1984); D. Moggridge, *Maynard Keynes: An Economist's Biography* (1992); Paul Davidson, *John Maynard Keynes* (2007); and R. Skidelsky, *John Maynard Keynes: Hopes Betrayed 1883–1920* (1983), and *John Maynard Keynes: The Economist as Saviour 1920–1937* (1992), and *John Maynard Keynes, Fighting for Britain 1937–1946* (2001). A single-volume abridgment, *John Maynard Keynes: Economist, Philosopher Statesman 1883–1946*, was published in 2003. Skidelsky's *Keynes: The Return of the Master* (2009) was a plea for his relevance to understand, and prescribe for, the slump of 2008–9. Anand Chandavarkar, *The Unexplored Keynes and Other Essays* (2009) offers an engaging account of Keynes's many-sided genius. Justyn Walsh, *Keynes and the Market* (2008) shows how Keynes's varied experience as an investor influenced his economic theories.

Theory

Only a tiny sample of a vast secondary literature can be given here. Paul Krugman, *Introduction to Keynes's The General Theory of Employment, Interest and Money* (2006) is a scintillating account of Keynes's central theory from a 'new Keynesian' standpoint. Michael Stewart, *Keynes and After* (3rd edn. 1986), is the most accessible introductory text. E. Eshag, *From Marshall to Keynes: An Essay on the*

Monetary Theory of the Cambridge School (1963), the classic account, needs to be supplemented by R. J. Bigg, *Cambridge and the Monetary Theory of Production* (1990). D. Patinkin, *Keynes's Monetary Thought: A Study of its Development* (1977), as well as his essay on Keynes in the *New Palgrave Dictionary of Economics*, ed. J. Eatwell, M. Milgate, and P. Newman (1987), are standard technical accounts. J. R. Hicks's *Critical Essays in Monetary Theory* (1967) has an illuminating 'Note on the Treatise (on Money)'. Richard Kahn, *The Making of Keynes's General Theory* (1984), is important first-hand testimony; G. L. S. Shackle, *The Years of High Theory: Invention and Tradition in Economic Thought 1926–39* (1967), is an excellent account of the 'double revolution' in Cambridge. Four stimulating interpretations of Keynes's theory are Tim Congdon, *Keynes, the Keynesians, and Monetarism* (2007); Gilles Dostaler, *Keynes and His Battles* (2007); A. H. Meltzer, *Keynes's Monetary Theory: A Different Interpretation* (1988); and Murray Milgate, *Capital and Employment: A Study of Keynes's Economics* (1982). Victoria Chick, *On Money, Method and Keynes: Selected Essays*, ed. Philip Arestis and Sheila Dow (1992), and Hyman P. Minsky, *John Maynard Keynes* (1975) are important interpretations from the post-Keynesian standpoint. P. Clarke, *The Keynesian Revolution in the Making 1924–1936* (1988) is essential reading; R. W. Dimand, *The Origins of the Keynesian Revolution* (1988) covers some of the same ground from a technical standpoint. P. V. Mini, *Keynes, Bloomsbury and The General Theory* (1991) is a stimulating, off-beat essay. John Williamson's essay, 'Keynes and the International Economic Order', in D. Worswick and J. Trevithik (eds.), *Keynes and the Modern World* (1983) is exemplary. Indispensable introductions to Keynes's epistemology are Anna M. Carabelli, *On Keynes's Method* (1988) and R. M. O'Donnell, *Keynes: Philosophy, Economics and Politics* (1989). Terence Hutchison, *On the Methodology of Economics and the Formalist Revolution* (2000) is an excellent account of how economics came to be 'mathematicized'. Taleb Nassim, *The Black Swan: The Impact of the Highly Improbable* (2007) shows up the fraudulence of most mathematical forecasting models.

Legacy

D. Patinkin, *Money, Interest and Prices: An Integration of Monetary and Value Theory* (1956), and the Hicks–Patinkin exchange which followed it in the *Economic Journal* (June 1957 and September 1959), were key to establishing the 'synthesis' between the neo-classical theorists and the policy Keynesians; an accommodation challenged by A. Leijonhufvud, *On Keynesian Economics and the Economics of Keynes* (1966). (See also Leijonhufvud's essay, *Keynes and the Classics* (Institute of Economic Affairs, 1969).) David Marquand, *The Unprincipled Society* (1988) offers a lively interpretation of 'Keynesian social democracy' in Britain; for the impact of Keynesian ideas in the United States, H. Stein, *The Fiscal Revolution in America* (1969) is the key text; for Keynes's influence on other countries, see Peter A. Hall (ed.), *The Political Power of Economic Ideas: Keynesianism Across Nations* (1989). Eric Roll, *The World After Keynes: An Examination of the Economic Order* (1968) is a standard offering from the 'golden age'. The crucial monetarist text is Milton Friedman's Presidential address to the American Economic Association, 29 December 1967, on 'The Role of Monetary Policy', published in the *American Economic Review* (March 1968), 1–17. The main text of 'new Keynesianism' is N. G. Mankiw and D. Romer (eds.), *New Keynesian Economics* (1991). Paul Davidson's *Money and the Real World* (2002 edition) is the statement of one of the leading 'post-Keynesians'. Henry Hazlitt (ed.), *The Critics of Keynesian Economics* (1960, 1977) is a collection of anti-Keynesian and sceptical essays. Arjo Klamer, *The New Classical Macroeconomics: Conversations with New Classical Economists and Their Opponents* (1984) is an indispensable window into the mindset of the Chicago School. Brian Snowdon and Howard R. Vane, *Modern Macroeconomics: Its Origins, Development and Current State* (2005) charts the 'decline and fall' of the original Keynesian revolution, and the rise of 'new Keynesianism' and the 'new classical economics', with interviews with some of the leading participants.

Index

'abnormal' unemployment 136
abstinence theory of economic
    progress 71
activities, wide-ranging 26, 33
aesthetic interests 18, 19, 40
Allsopp, Christopher 126
Anglocentrism 8
'animal spirits' investment theory
    25, 159
anti-elitism, Labour party 53
artistic interests 18, 19, 40
Arts Council chairmanship 37, 40
automatic mechanisms, absence
    of 31

Bagehot, Walter 60
balance of payments
    adjustment 160-1
Baldwin, Stanley 51, 69, 155
'banana parable' 74, 82
bancor balances 36
bank lending 66
banking crisis, 1914 20, 60
banking crisis, 2008-9 147, 149
    causes 152-3
    role of global imbalances 163
    stimulus packages 154-6
banking policy 70
Banking Policy and the Price Level
    (1926), Dennis Robertson 66

banking system reforms 164
benevolence 8
Besusan-Butt, James 2
Blackett, Basil 22
Bloomsbury Group 18, 24
Brand, Robert 117
Bretton Woods Agreement 36,
    108, 115, 119, 127, 145, 161
Bretton Woods II 162
'brigand powers', Germany and
    Italy as 110-11
British National Plan (1965) 132
broad monetarism 63
Brown, Florence Ada *see* Keynes,
    Florence Ada
budget deficits, in definition of
    Keynesian Revolution 126
Burke, Edmund, Keynes's essay
    on 45-9
business-cycle theory 66

calculable future, Keynes's
    mistrust 87
Callaghan, James 124
Cambridge Apostles 17-18
Cambridge Arts Theatre 40
Cambridge Circus 32
Cambridge University
    investment Bursarship 24
    teaching duties 24

Cambridge University (*continued*)
undergraduate studies 17–18
Cambridge upbringing 15–16
Can Lloyd George Do it? (1929) 31,
69, 85, 155
capital goods, uncertainty
analysis 73
capitalism, Keynes's legacy 123
capitalistic individualism 14
career choice 9
cash balances form of quantity
theory 56, 57
Cassel, Gustav 61
causal chains, Keynes's use 88–9
central banking theory 60
Champeronowne, David 96
China, transition from
Communism 142
Churchill, Winston 29
return to gold standard 65
Clark, Kenneth 4
Clarke, Peter, *The Keynesian
Revolution in the Making* 68
class 53
classical economics, revival 146
'classical theory', relationship to
'general theory' 94–9
Clearing Union plan (1941) 36,
113–14, 116, 117, 159, 161
Clemenceau, Georges 23
cleverness 16
Coddington, Alan 139
Communism, fall of 142, 146
company mergers, British National
Plan (1965) 132
conscientious objection 21
conscription, arguments
against 20–1
conservatism 6, 48, 49
Conservatism, Keynes's view 51
constant price models 138
Consultative Committee, to Chancellor of Exchequer (1940) 34
consumption, stimulation of 166
consumption function 90

consumption function/multiplier
analysis 69, 97–8
contemporaries 3
coronary thrombosis (1937) 34
Council for the Encouragement of
Music and the Arts (CEMA)
chairmanship 37
Crafts, N.F.R. and Woodward,
N. 127
credit creation 60, 63
'credit cycle' investment theory 25
creditor countries 160–1
curiosity 7
cyclical stability 124, 144

Dalton, Hugh 117
Davenport, Nicholas 11–12
'Day of Judgement' reflections 100
De Contemptu Mundi , Bernard of
Cluny 37
'dear money' policy 137
death 37
death duties 47
deferred earnings scheme 35, 104–6
definitions in *The General
Theory* 89–90
deflationary policies 65, 120, 163–4
demand, relationship to
unemployment 143
demand and supply, theory of 79, 81
see also Say's law
demand expansion 130
demand management 131–2,
138–9, 141
democracy 48–9
depression
causes 73
see also slump
devaluation, British National Plan
(1965) 132
developmental economics 123–4
directorships of investment and
insurance companies 24
disequilibrium theories 123
domestic monetary control 29

Dow, Christopher 139
duty, sense of 5, 39, 41

econometrics 11, 43, 123
    limitations 149–51, 168
Economic Advisory Council
        membership 24, 31, 76
economic blocs 111, 118, 119
*Economic Consequences of
        Mr. Churchill* (1925) 29, 65
*Economic Consequences of the
        Peace* (1919) 22–3, 27, 61
economic history, theory of 99–100
Economic Journal , editorship 24
economic laws 10
*Economic Possibilities for our
        Grandchildren* (1930) 53
economic theories, impact on
        government policies 125–6
economics, philosophy of 10–11
economist, Keynes as 10
economists, qualities of 10
education
    Cambridge University 17–18
    Eton 6, 16
effective demand, theory of 87
efficiency 6–7, 26
'efficiency wages' 74, 75
Efficient Market Hypothesis 149,
        152
eloquence 115
employment
    'classical' account 94–5
    effect on prices 96–7
    relationship to investment 82
    White Paper on Employment
        Policy (1944) 107
    see also loan-financed
        public works programme;
        unemployment
Employment, General Law of 84
employment multiplier 70
employment-raising policy 95–6
End of Laissez-Faire, The 30, 50
epitaph 37

equilibrium terms of trade 76
equilibrium theory 147, 153–4
equity, principle of 45
Essays in Biography (1933) 32
Essays in Persuasion (1931) 32
ethical beliefs 38–40
Eton education 6, 16
European Economic
        Community 130
European 'New Order' proposal
        (1940) 112
'euthanasia of the rentier' 48, 100
exchange rates 27, 28, 108–10, 160–1
    Bretton Woods Agreement 161
    Clearing Union plan 36, 161
    management of 167
    stability 29, 62
expectational function 128
expectations, uncertain 148, 151–2
expediency, political 45
expenditure, determination of 83–4
expertise, respect for 8

'faithfulness' investment theory 25
Falk, Oswald 2, 24–5
family allowances 104
family background 5, 9, 14–16
fatigue 7
financial collapse (1931) 31–2
financial instability 148–9
First World War 4, 20–2
    'forced saving' 67
fiscal policy use, 1960s 129
Fisher, Irving, quantity theory of
        money 56–7
flexible wages 74
'forced saving' 67
forces of recovery 99
foreign investment and lending 68
Foxwell, Herbert 15
free society, application of Keynes's
        theories 140
free trade 111, 145
    European fears 130
    United States policy 111, 114

Index

frequency theory 42
Friedman, Milton 122, 124, 142, 144
frugality 5
full employment, definition 135–6
Fundamental Equations 71, 75, 81
Funk, Walther, European 'New Order' proposal (1940) 112
future, fears for 26–7
future goods 46

gambling 11–12
General Law of Employment 84
General Strike (1926) 29–30
   Keynes's sympathies 50
General Theory of Employment, Interest, and Money (1936) 1, 2, 12, 32–3, 44, 87–8
   analytical kernel 90
   analytical method 88–9
   definitions 89–90
   as equilibrium theory 147
   fundamental units 82–4
   historical perspective 122
   influence 33–4
   influence of world slump 80–1
   legacy 123
   link with *Treatise on Money* 79
   nature of unemployment 135–6
   organization 88
   on public spending 135
   restatement (1937) 101–2
General Theory of Employment (1937) 148
generalization 12–13, 30–1
German government, Keynes as unofficial adviser 28
German reparations 22–3, 27, 68
Gilpin, A.C. 32
global imbalances 159–62
   as cause of economic meltdown 163
global reserves, reduction 166–7
globalization 141, 146
   reform of international monetary system 166–7

gold standard 127, 161–2
   collapse 119
   Harry Dexter White's plan 114–15
   Keynes' rejection 28–9, 31, 62–3
   Keynes's response to disintegration 108
   price stabilization 58–9
   proposed modifications 108, 109
   return to (1925) 65
golden age, 1950s–1960s 125
   contribution of technological progress 127
   effect of Keynesian policy 129–33
   role of United States 127–8
good actions 39
goodness, judgement of 40
government management of the economy 144, 146, 164, 168–9
   impact of economic theories 125–6
   investment stimulation 164–6
   printing money 155–6, 158
   reform of international monetary system 166–7
   stimulation of consumption 165
Grant, Duncan 18, 21
Great Depression (1929–33) 13, 26–7, 31–2
'Great Moderation' 147
'great society' spending programmes 129–30
Greenspan, Alan 163
growth 122
   1950's–1960's 131–3

Harrod, Roy 10–11, 33, 98, 124
Hawtrey, Ralph 32, 68–9, 81, 155
Hayek, F.A. 32
health problems 34
Henderson, Hubert 24, 31, 69, 107
hereditary principle 51
Hicks, John 101, 127
historical background 3–4, 13, 14
Hitler, Adolf 27

Keynes's opinion 110–11
hoarding 5
homosexuality 18
housing boom, collapse 163
'How Far are Bankers Responsible for the Alterations of Crisis and Depression?' (1913) 60
'How to Avoid a Slump' *Times* articles (1937) 34
How to Pay for the War (1939) 35, 103–4, 105
Hull, Cordell 111
Hutchinson, Terence 139

imagination, scientific 11
impoverishment as 'nature's cure' 74
income/expenditure model 83–6, 147–8
incomes policies 139
    1970s 133
inconsistency 4
India, as sink of precious metals 159–60
India Office employment 17
Indian Currency and Finance (1913) 19, 59, 161–2
indifference, principle of 41
inductive method, objections to 43
industrialization, state-led 131
inflation 60–1
    1960s–1970s 133
    1970s 125
    'forced saving' 66–7
    Keynes's proposed cure 137
    Phillips Curve 138
inflation tax 135
inflationary gap, Second World War 104–5
intellect 4–5, 7, 9
Intelligentsia of Great Britain, The, Dmitri, Mirsky 54
inter-Ally war debts 23
Interest and Prices, Knut Wicksell 59
interest rate

adjustment 84
    determination of 92–3, 98
    roles 73
    in stimulation of investment 164–5
international economy, 'Keynes Plan' 107–12
International Monetary Fund 36, 37
    inauguration 161
    Special Drawing Rights 162, 167
international monetary system, reform 166–7
international trade
    discrimination against United States 111–12
    economic blocs 111, 118
    US free trade policy 111, 114
intolerance 8
intuitive reasoning 11, 38, 42, 168
investment
    'animal spirits' theory 25, 159
    definition 89
    instability 148
    link to savings 70, 73
    marginal efficiency of capital (MEC) 153
    relationship to volume of employment 82
    socialization of 50, 165
    stimulation of 164–6
    volatility 91–2
investment demand 90
investment theories 25, 44
investment yields, uncertainty 151–2, 157
'iron ration' 104
IS/LM curves 101

Japan, deficit financing 131
Johnston, Thomas 52
Johnston, W.E. 15
Joplin, Thomas 67
journalism 25

Kahn, Richard 30, 32, 70, 77, 85–6, 136
'key' currency, dollar as 162
Keynes, Florence Ada (née Brown, mother) 15
Keynes, John Neville (father) 14–15
'Keynes Plans' 103
  Clearing Union 113–14
  deferred earnings scheme 104–6
  international economy 107–12
'Keynesian' budgets 105
Keynesian Revolution 83, 101
  as barrier to new ideas 134
  continuation after Keynes's death 122–3
  death of 124, 140–1, 146
  definition 126–7
  effect on golden age 129–33
  expectational function 128
  future prospects 141–2
  historical perspective 122, 125, 145
  impact on government policies 125–6
  social democratic phase 129
Keynesian Revolution in the Making, The, Peter Clarke 68
knowledge, love of 39

Labour Party, Keynes's view 30, 52–3
labour shortages, Europe 130
Lawson, Nigel 120
leakages 86
Leffingwell, Russell 2
legacy 120–1, 123–4
  death of Keynesian Revolution 124
Leijonhufvud, Axel 123, 154
Lend–Lease scheme (1940) 112–13, 114
  cancellation 117
Lerner, Abba 138
Liberal Industrial Inquiry (1927–8) 30
Liberalism 23, 49–51

liquidity preference 73, 90, 92–3, 102, 153, 159
liquidity traps 93, 157–8
Lloyd George, David 21, 30
loan agreement with US (1945) 117–18
loanable-funds theory of interest rate 98
loan-financed public works programme 31, 68–70, 78, 85, 155
Lombard Street, Walter Bagehot 60
London life 24
Lopokova, Lydia 7, 10, 25–6
Lucas, Robert 142, 154

Macmillan Committee on Finance and Industry 31, 76–8
macroeconomic models 142–3
macroeconomics 123, 124
Malthus, Thomas, Keynes's essay on 10
Manchester Guardian Commercial, Reconstruction Supplements 27
'Manchester system' 100
marginal efficiency of capital (MEC) 91, 153
market psychology, factors of 83–4
Marquand, David 129
marriage to Lydia Lopokova 25–6
Marshall, Alfred 15
  Keynes's essay on 9–10
  quantity theory of money 56, 57
Martin, Kingsley 4
'masks' 7–8
mathematical forecasts, limitations 150–1, 168
Matthews, R.C.O. 126
McDonald, Ramsay 31
McKenna, Reginald 20
Meade, James 2, 105, 115
Means to Prosperity, The (1933) 32, 86
Melchior, Carl 28

Keynes

memorial service 37
method of expectations 89
Middle Way 30, 105–6
Mirsky, Dmitri, *The Intelligentsia of Great Britain* 54
'misery index', 1970s 133
'mispricing of risk' 149
'mixed goods', G.E. Moore 40
monetarism 120–1, 142–3
  narrow 63
monetary nationalism 75
monetary policy 66, 80, 102
  main object 75
  printing money 155–6, 158
  public confidence 93
  in stimulation of investment 164–5
money
  quantity theory 55–8
  as store of wealth 90
money illusion 96
money income, definition in *Treatise on Money* 71
moneymaking 25
money-wages 97
  effect of reductions 95–6
Moore, G.E. 17, 18, 38–41
moral philosophy 17, 18
moral risk 43, 46
multiplier theory 32, 70, 77, 85–7, 147
Munich settlement 111

narrow monetarism 63
Nation and Atheneum (journal) 24
national finance systems 109, 141
National government (1931) 31–2
National Mutual Life Assurance Company 24
national self-sufficiency 33
'natural' rate of interest 59
'natural rate of unemployment 143
'nature's cure', impoverishment as 74
Nazism, Keynes's opinion 110

negotiating skills 115–16
'neo-Malthusian' thinking 27
'new Keynesians' 143
Newton, Isaac, Keynes's essay on 11
Nicolson, Harold 112
Niemeyer, Otto 17
Non-Accelerating Inflation Rate of Unemployment (NAIRU) 136–7
Nonconformist background 6
nonconformity 5
'normal' unemployment 136

object of desire, money as 1
oil-price rises, 1970s 129, 133
optimism 2, 13
organic unity principle 40
original thinking, Keynes's views on 87
output, determination of 83
output gap, 1950's 130
output growth 131–2
over-ambition 121–2
  in 1960s 133
overwork 7
Oxbridge, curse of 8

paradox of thrift 91
Paris Peace Conference 22
patriotism 5
'Paying for the War' (1939) 103–4
Pearson, Karl 19
peerage 34
personal saving leakage 86
philanthropy 40
Phillips Curve 138, 143
philosophy of practice 38
  G.E. Moore's influence 38–41
  politics 45–54
  theory of probability 41–4
Pigou, Arthur 99, 123
  monetary equation 63–4
  Theory of Unemployment (1933) 94, 95
political economy 164–7

political naïvety 139–40
political theory 45–54
politicians, motivation 140
politics, Middle Way 105–6
'portable' Keynesian model 101
Prebisch, Raoul 131
present goods 46
price reduction, causes 70
price stability 61–3, 64, 124, 137
price stabilization 58
prices, effect of rising
    employment 96–7
Principia Ethica, G.E. Moore 17,
    38–41
printing money 155–6, 158
probability
    Keynes's dissertation 9, 19, 41, 44
    theory of 41–4
productivity growth 131–2
profits, definition in *Treatise on
    Money* 71–2
property rights 47–8
protection, as remedy for
    slump 76, 77–8
psychology of stock exchange 73, 92
public spending 135
    as engine of growth 132
    rise in 1960's 129
public works policy, Lloyd
    George 31, 68–70, 78, 85, 155
public–private partnerships 165
purchasing power parity theory of
    exchanges 61

quantitative easing 155–6, 158
quantity theory of money 55–8,
    63–4, 97, 138
    Milton Friedman's
        restatement 124
    transactions version 68

rationality of means 41–3, 47
rationing 106
redistribution of spending
    power 100

'Relation of Home Investment to
    Unemployment, The' (1931),
    Richard Kahn 85
religion 3, 4, 5, 17
    Keynes's rejection 38
reserve accumulation, global
    imbalances 159–61
reserves, reduction 166–7
risk, mispricing of 149
risk management 149
    distinction from uncertainty 149
Robbins, Lionel 115–16
Robertson, Dennis 12, 30, 32, 66,
    82, 98–9
Robertson, H.M. 30
Robinson, Joan and Austin 30
Roosevelt, Franklin D. 109, 110
    Lend–Lease scheme 112–13
    open letter to (1933) 8–9
rudeness 8–9, 22, 115
Russell, Bertrand 4, 7

Sargent, Thomas 142
saving
    definition 72, 89
    link to investment 70, 73
    paradox of thrift 91
saving–investment disequilibrium
    model 73–6, 81–2
savings
    'forced' 67
    use to buy existing assets 67–8
Say's Law 83, 84, 89
    Keynes's denial of 97–8
Schachtian devices 113
school education 6
scientific imagination 11
Second World War 34–5, 114
    Anglo–American
        agreement 115–16
    current account deficit 116–17
    deferred earnings scheme 104–6
    Lend–Lease scheme 112–13
    outbreak 103–4
    United States involvement 111, 114

secular stagnation thesis 100, 130
self-government 48–9
self-hatred 7
self-regulation of markets 146, 148, 168
semi-inflation 138
sermons, economic essays as 6
'short-period' analysis 88, 89
Sidgwick, Henry 15
Singer, Kurt 5, 9, 13, 30
slump
    impact on Keynes's thinking 80–1
    remedies for 76–8
    see also depression; Great depression
slumpfation, 1970s 125, 133–4
Smith, Adam 128
Snowden, Philip 76
social democratic phase of Keynesianism 129
social interactions 7–8
social justice 50
social philosophy 122
social policy 106, 141
social reform, ethical considerations 40
social security benefits 10
social sympathies 6, 16
socialisation of investment 100
socialism 23
    Keynes's view 52–3
socialization of investment 50, 165
socialized capitalism 50
Soviet states, transition from Communism 142
Special Drawing Rights (SDRs) 162, 167
speculation 25
speculative instinct 11–12
Sraffa, Piero 30
Stabilization Fund, modified gold standard 114–15
stable equilibrium 84–5
state-led industrialization 131
states of mind 39–40

statistics
    intuitive use of 11
    limitations 149–51, 168
    scepticism about 19–20, 43
Stein, Herbert 8–9
Sterling Area 107, 116, 117, 119
stereotypes 1–2
Stewart, Walter 8
stimulus packages 154–6
stock exchange, psychology of 73, 92
Strachey, Lytton 18
structural maladjustment 121
structure of production 88
successive over-emphasis 12
'suction pump' effect, wealth distribution 166
'super-sovereign reserve currency' 167
supply constraints 133, 139

tariff protection 77
Tarshis, Lorie 2
tax cuts 164
technological progress, contribution towards 'golden age' 127
'technological' unemployment 122
Theory of Unemployment (1933) 95
thrift, paradox of 91
Tilton, East Sussex home 26
Tobin, James 130
'Tobin' tax 167
Tomlinson, Jim 126
total income, definition 82
Tract on Monetary Reform, A (1923) 28–9, 47–8, 61–5, 122
transactions view of money 56, 68
transmission mechanism, money to prices 58
Treasury career (1915–19) 20–2
Treasury office 1940s 34
'Treasury View' (1928–9) 68
Treatise on Money (1930) 30–1, 68, 70–5, 122, 157
    link with General Theory 79

Treatise on Probability (1921) 9,
      19, 41, 44
truth, pursuit of 46–7
Tuesday Club 24

uncertainty 1, 4, 44–5, 102, 147–8
      as cause of unemployment
            153–4
      as condition for liquidity
            preference 92–3
      distinction from risk 149
      effects on business beha-
            viour 64–5
      of expectations 148
      financial instability 148–9
      investment yields 151–2
      limited applicability of
            econometrics 149–51
      and liquidity preference 90, 157
      modelling 168
underemployment equilibrium 28
undergraduate studies,
      Cambridge 17–18
unemployment 14
      1920s 28
      1980s 141
      causes 70, 95–6, 143, 153–4, 163
      loan-financed public works
            programme 68–70
      nature of 135–7
      as price for reduction of
            inflation 137
      as result of deflationary policies
            120
      structural 121
      'technological' 122
      in United States 130
      see also employment
United States
      American loan negotiations
            (1945) 36–7
      financial dependence on 21–2,
            23, 107–8
      International Monetary Fund
            inauguration 37

Keynes's opinion of 22, 110
Lend–Lease scheme 112–13
loan negotiations (1945) 36–7
post-war missions 34–5, 117–18
reserve accumulation 160–1
role in golden age 127–8
unbalanced creditor position
      108, 111, 112, 119
unemployment 130
usury 48
utilitarianism 45
utopianism 53

Victorian values 5, 6, 15, 17
vigilant observation 10, 11
Vinson, Frederick 9
voluntary unemployment 136

wage adjustment 83
wage costs, impact of return to gold
      standard 29
wage flexibility 74
wage pressure 63
wages explosion 133
Wall Street, bull market (1927–9) 68
war, hatred of 20–1
war debts 23
Ward, James 15
Warming, Jens 86
wartime finance 35
wealth, redistribution of 47–8, 50
wealth distribution, 'suction pump'
      effect 166
Webb, Beatrice 2
weight of argument 43
White, Harry Dexter 115
      modified gold standard
            plan 114–15
White Paper on Employment
      Policy (1944) 107
Wicksell, Knut 58–9
Wilson, Woodrow 23
Wood, Kingsley 35, 105
Woolf, Virginia 4, 7
work habits 6–7

Keynes